INSIDE SALES
PREDICTABILITY

Seven insider secrets to building a **predictable and scalable real estate business** with inside sales

By
MICHAEL REESE

Cover design: Prasad.ktn (99designs) and Karin Carroll

Cover image: © lightwise (123rf.com)

ISBN 978-1539061069

Printed by CreateSpace

Available from Amazon.com and other online and retail outlets

TABLE OF CONTENTS

FOREWORD by Jay Kinder

"There's got to be a better way!"

We have all reached a point in our real estate businesses where we take a deep breath, lean back in our office chair, and mumble that phrase.

For me that moment came at a time when most people would say I was very successful. I was closing, without any real predictability, five to eight transactions a month and working 12 hours a day, including weekends.

I'd gotten off the real estate roller coaster, but I was paying for it both physically and emotionally. I knew that I could make the calls and generate listing appointments, but the whirlwind in my business kept making it harder and harder to keep up with my calls.

I'd heard of a few agents who had hired an Inside Sales Associate (ISA), but I didn't really know exactly how to go about it. I didn't know who I was looking for, nor did I have a clue about setting expectations, roles and responsibilities, compensation, onboarding for success, efficiency, reporting, and a host of other things you need to know in order to successfully hire, onboard, and train an ISA.

The process can be rife with pitfalls, but you will learn how to avoid all of them in this book.

You can be successful with an ISA hire even if you make some of the mistakes that I made. Most of the top agents and teams that have ISAs have them taking inbound and making some outbound calls (you are likely guilty of doing this yourself if you've ever had an ISA).

Once you get really good at delegating, you may also be guilty of giving your ISA more responsibility related to creating files, doing paperwork, etc., instead of making calls. It's easy to justify doing this, but it really flies in the face of what you've hired your ISA to do for you.

This book reveals a much bigger, much more predictable, and much more profitable way to utilize an ISA or multiple ISAs in your business... without diluting their efficacy with extraneous activities.

One quote I've heard Michael say many times is, "Success is just as hard to deal with as failure," and at this point in your real estate career, likely nothing could be truer. And if it's success you seek—whether you are looking to hire your first ISA or you want to build a call center with 100 ISAs to run your expanding empire—you have the game plan for success in your hands.

Look, I've known Michael for 18 years. In fact, I'm one of the reasons Michael got into real estate, and I watched in amazement as he built his business to over $1 million in GCI by his third year. In his fifth year he listed over 360 homes.

He was a beast.

Since then, he and I have built a company that has coached and trained agents on how to build successful businesses. Also, we've helped thousands of agents get past 100 transactions, with many of them building multimillion-dollar empires.

Over the years of doing this, we learned there is one catalyst to your real estate success that is irrefutable: your ability to systematically and predictably generate listings. We've seen this countless times in our own real estate businesses and in those of our coaching clients.

In almost every one of those multimillion-dollar businesses, you would find two critical ingredients:

At some point the team leaders made the calls.
At some point along the way, they added the leverage of an ISA.

We have always known that this was an incredible point of leverage in your business, but what you are about to learn in this book about ISAs has never been shared before.

Here's an example of what I'm talking about.

When you attempt to scale your ISA department you quickly learn what works and what doesn't. For the purposes of clarity, scaling describes your business' capability to grapple with—and perform under—an ever-increasing workload. A business that scales properly will be able to sustain or even increase its level of performance and productivity when taxed by a larger workload.

What that means in terms of your ISA is this: When you have one ISA making outbound calls you might not freak out if your "contacted rate" is low. When you have 10, a low contact rate could crater your business.

As well, you probably won't run out of leads to call if you have one ISA handling your calls. If you have 10, you better have enough data and leads to call or inefficiency will eat your lunch.

In our business, we faced a similar scaling challenge.

Michael wanted to prove that he could deliver four to five listings a month, every month, in a predefined geographic area. Generally this would happen for one agent who we would partner with in a geographic location ranging in population from 150,000 to 350,000.

The problem that Michael was trying to solve wasn't just hiring and training one ISA. He needed to build a machine comprised of multiple ISAs that could deliver, with precision, a number of quality listing appointments in very targeted areas for multiple partners.

This book is the result of what he learned in his effort to build an outbound ISA department, which at the same time had Michael tapping into the biggest opportunity we have seen in years.

This book reveals the secret to hiring, training, compensating, leading, and managing one or one hundred ISAs. More importantly, it gives you the blueprint to predictably generate listings for you, your team, or for your expansion team.

We've sold literally thousands of homes (my estimate would be over 5,000 at the time of my writing this) and nothing has been more shocking than the impact of what you will learn from the pages that follow.

To give you perspective on the power of what you're about to learn, consider this: In the last 12 months, Michael built a brokerage and grew it from 34 to 240 deals using outbound ISAs at the core of the strategy.

That brokerage is now pacing for over 400 deals in its second year.

I've never seen anything like that before.

What you are reading isn't theory, it's been proven and documented in the pages you are about to read.

My suggestion to you is to take this book, find a quiet place, and read it in its entirety.

Then go implement everything in it as prescribed.

In the end, remember this: "If you want to go fast, go alone. If you want to go farther, go together." – African Proverb

Enjoy!

Jay Kinder

ACKNOWLEDGEMENTS

There are a number of people I'd like to thank for helping make this book possible.

To my partner and brother JAY KINDER. I would like to thank Jay for getting me into the business. He always pushed me to raise my standards as it related to selecting talent and hiring the right person in this department. Jay is always pushing me to remember the importance of high-level feedback loops and proper training when building out any department. He's the one person who has always been aligned and committed to finding a better way and stretching me so I make sure to think of "all the ways to accomplish the goal".

To JOHN KITCHENS for always helping us staying focused on the importance of maintaining great leadership and perpetuating a culture of account-ability. His unique point of view from his experience with managing and leading ISA's was very instrumental in the creation of this book. John's in-depth knowledge of all the potential failures and pitfalls of building an ISA department helped shape this book into the masterpiece I feel it is today.

To ALEX PIECH for running our Dallas HUB and working tirelessly to help implement the ISA department that was the case study for much of what's in this book. His contributions to our business and this book are invaluable.

To KARIN CARROLL for spending a considerable amount of time with me on the phone at all hours of the day to ensure that the framework of our ISA department is solid and impenetrable. Throughout our journey we've had to go outside of our industry to find all the possible solutions to the problems that stood in our way. Karin's ability to make the complicated simple made this entire project rewarding and fun. Without her, innovating the best solutions to scale this department would not have happened.

To JEFF ABRAMS for crunching every number possible from our ISAs' efforts to give me the guidance and information I need to help successfully grow our business.

To WOODS DAVIS for his marketing and business genius and his daily contributions to making our business bigger and better every day.

To ZACH BOWERS for conquering some of the biggest data science hurdles we faced, and building the data delivery machine to drive our inside sales predictability.

To MIKE ODDO for grabbing hold of the vision and working with us to create a platform to deliver the highest level of value to our industry.

To KYLE DAVIS for taking the time to read a draft of this book and give us an honest assessment of what needed to be improved.

To ALBIE STASEK for being transparent and open about his experience in hiring and managing ISAs in an effort to shorten the learning curve for us.

To BRETT JENNINGS for being willing to take what he's learned from us in the ISA department and then reporting his research and results to us so we could learn from him, too.

Finally, I want to thank MR. BRESSLER for his contribution to this book. He not only helped organize all the thoughts to make this book a reality, but he also helped make each individual ISA successful. He made sure that each ISA possessed every possible skill needed to be successful as we built the ISA department. He is ALWAYS willing to add value; morning, day, or night. He has always possessed a ride or die attitude and that has helped shape the amazing team of individuals we now have as ISAs.

INTRODUCTION

I was able to see what I wanted to do, I could see the
opportunity, even when others could not, and I stayed
committed to doing it and doing it well, no matter what.
– Magic Johnson

The "Market Maker" and the "Market Maker Mindset"

When writing a book about business, there are a couple of approaches you can take: 1) provide mass amounts of theory and leave the readers to determine how much of what they've read applies to them and then have them try to figure out how to apply what's been taught to their business, or 2), be direct in explaining who is the audience for your book and give them "the handles to the luggage" (so to speak) so they can use what you've taught in a very practical way.

For this book, I chose the second option.

My friends, this book is for you, the Market Makers of the real estate industry. It's for the people in real estate who look for the opportunity beyond the opportunity to grow their business; individuals who see that there's more to creating and running a business than what the market brings to them on a day-over-day basis.

What is a Market Maker?

In stock trading, a Market Maker is a bank or trading organization that is prepared each trading day to offer a solid "ask" and "bid" cost for virtually any security. A Market Maker will readily buy and sell stocks whether or not it has a vendor standing by with whom to do business. In doing this, it is literally making a market for a security where there may be none at the time. Market Makers reduce the amount of time it takes for sellers and buyers to work out a deal, increase liquidity and reduce the cost associated with buying and selling stocks.

As a Market Maker in the real estate industry, you're continually finding and creating ways to help buyers and sellers get things done faster, easier and in as financially advantageous a position as possible.

Also, you're laser focused on finding ways to generate more listing and buyer opportunities to create a larger and more profitable business – literally finding ways to make something where there is currently nothing – all while helping your clients and employees achieve their goals by choosing to work with you.

The Market Maker Mindset

The key to achieving great results in being a Market Maker is your laser focus on **creating additional opportunity where there appears to be**

none. It's a mindset that sees no boundaries on how and where new business can be found. And, it's all rooted in using your labor dollar creatively enough to hire ISAs to unearth these additional opportunities so you can take advantage of them.

Having a Market Maker Mindset means you look beyond only calling expireds, withdrawns and FSBOs on a daily basis. It means you do more than having your ISAs handle only inbound calls. As a Market Maker, you use your ISAs to execute an outbound calling strategy that searches in the nooks and crannies of the vast landscape of listing opportunities where other agents don't even bother to look.

Market Makers look to capture every listing opportunity in their farm market, including FSBOs, current expireds, past expireds and every other seller deal they can uncover.

Market Makers secure and develop relationships with divorce, probate, estate and bankruptcy attorneys to generate a steady-stream of highly-qualified, highly-loyal seller prospects.

Market Makers know that they can't rely just on what comes to them; they have a mindset that leads them to searching under every rock for consistent and predictable listing opportunities.

Market Makers focus only on what's in their control...but they know that generating a predictable pipeline of listing opportunities (using an outbound ISA strategy) is completely within their control.

3

Let's Stay in Touch

If you like what I've shared with you in this book, you can receive a concise weekly email with recordings of our ISAs making a full range of expired calls including expireds, withdrawns, FSBOs, home evaluation leads, circle prospecting and many other lead sources. Each email will have a headline stating THIS WEEK'S CALL and it will include a brief summary and link to the call. For those who would like to get access to these weekly call recordings and dig deeper on improving conversion, simply send an email to *michael@insidesalespredictability.com* and put WEEKLY CALLS in the subject line. We'll add you to our expanding list of Market Makers.

OVERVIEW

Let's face it, building a successful inside sales department isn't brain surgery...but it can certainly feel like it at times.

And no matter what stage you are at in your real estate career, the thought of bringing on an Inside Sales Associate (ISA)—or getting the one you have to produce consistently—makes *your* brain feel like it's going to be damaged permanently as you try to make it happen.

If this describes you, I have some good news for you.

In this book, I take the mystery out of how to nail implementing inside sales within your business—whether you want or have one ISA or a hundred ISAs—and turn it into…

…an invisible sales machine that provides a predictable pipeline of appointments, listings and profits for your real estate business for years to come.

And at the same time, it gives your brain a bit of a break because anyone who's committed to following what I've outlined in this book can have amazing results with an ISA.

An ISA is a Market Maker; a skilled salesperson who understands the nuances of building relationships and selling over the phone. Having an ISA gives you the bandwidth you need to get in front of more sellers—do more business—knowing that high-quality prospecting calls are being made each day to fill your pipeline with legitimate sales opportunities.

An ISA is a monstrous asset to your team.

The ultimate prize, though, is a real estate enterprise that offers you tremendous predictability and scalability. More specifically, by using the information provided in this book, you'll be able to generate consistent listing appointments and know month over month which prospects in your pipeline are likely to become legitimate listing opportunities. More importantly, you'll find out how to put them in your pipeline steadily and frequently.

Additionally, you'll discover how to create a profitable business with huge growth potential that isn't dependent on just you, rather, it will come as a result of segmenting the key duties in your sales sequence and putting highly skilled talent in charge of handling them.

What I share here will help you enjoy a quality of life and a standard of living that, up until today, has been reserved for the top one to two percent of agents in world. In fact, you'll become the dominant listing agent in your marketplace which means motivated sellers will seek you out to list their homes because you are the "go-to" agent in the area.

This enhanced presence in your market will also lead to a much larger listing inventory of homes that sell fast and for top dollar, giving you access to the financial ammunition to create a business and life that affords you the time to do what you want when you want to—without being a slave to your real estate business.

It can—and will—change your life.

Results Not Rhetoric

In my world, distinction leads to clarity and clarity leads to power. And in order to have the power to get great results, you can't just talk a good game...you need to play the game and play it like a world champion. To play the game and win, you must do the right things in the right order to avoid the pitfalls and mistakes that many other agents experience when trying to master the ISA process.

Now, the road to building a successful inside sales department can be treacherous, so in order to determine what to do so you can avoid making huge, life-altering mistakes along the way, it's beneficial that we help you make some distinctions and get clear on where you are at this very moment.

To make this easy, I've broken it down into three very distinct stages:

- **Stage 1**: You want/need an ISA and you're either thinking about hiring one or you're in the process of hiring one. You may or may not have had an ISA in the past or you may or may not have used a virtual ISA or US-based prospecting service. If you did outsource the job, you likely did so with little or no luck.

- **Stage 2**: You have an ISA and you want better and more consistent results from the person you've brought on board. You're fairly confident that you hired the right person, but things have been going in fits and starts, and the quality and quantity of your listing appointments aren't where you want them to be.

- **Stage 3**: You have an ISA and you're ready to bring on a number of ISAs to create a predictable, lead generation and conversion machine. Business is moving along at a good clip and you feel that you have things pretty well figured out, but you need the blueprint for scaling your inside sales operation to take it to the next level.

Now that you know the stage in which you fit, you'll be able to apply to your current business model to what I'm going to share with you in this book and get predictable results faster than you ever dreamed possible. But before we buckle up for liftoff, I want to talk about the one thing you must consider before rolling up your sleeves and getting your hands dirty with mastering the ISA process.

Putting a Model to Work

When creating a successful business, there are some assumptions you need to make in order to ensure you're headed in the right direction. Yes, you will make some WAGs (wild-ass guesses) along the way, but in order to get great results, you need to follow a solid model that is rooted in educated assumptions.

In 1994, world-famous management consultant, Peter Drucker, crafted his *Theory of the business* and defined a model as "[*a set of*] *assumptions about what a company gets paid for—assumptions about what a business will and won't do.*"

Interestingly enough, a model is not about the money, it's about using assumptions to chart a course toward a specific goal. More precisely, it's about charting and following the course and then taking the lessons you learn along the way to make changes and improvements. These changes and improvements lead to you getting better results, faster and with less money spent along the way. The ideal outcome of a properly followed model is a business that creates a predictable pipeline of sales and becomes a cash-producing machine.

Within the main business model are smaller models that use the same strategy—assumptions, well-defined activities, and metrics—to achieve specific outcomes. In our business, we created a model for the ISA department and process and we started with a list of assumptions that pertained to the activities and behaviors in which we expected the ISAs to engage.

Some of our assumptions about the ISA were:

- How many dials would be made
- How many nurtures would be created
- How many appointments would be set
- How many conversions would there be from dial to nurture, dial to appointment, and nurture to appointment (What would that cycle look like?)
- How many of those appointments would result in how many deals

Once we made these assumptions, we then implemented a solid system of data delivery and reporting mechanisms through a centralized hub (all of which will be detailed later in this book) to verify the operating metrics.

This tracking process lets us know if we're on pace to accomplish what we thought we would through our initial set of assumptions. When we were on pace, our assumptions were on point and we continued with the same behaviors and activities to create a repeatable system that we could rely upon to produce consistent results day in and day out.

If our assumptions were wrong, we found out where the choke point was and then made adjustments to the activities, behaviors, data sets, personnel—even the assumptions—in order to get the results that gave us the predictability we wanted and needed.

By following the model, we were able to solve bottlenecks and get better results much faster than if we were simply taking stabs in the dark. Lastly, we saved a tremendous amount of time and money by not continuing to make mistakes that we would be able to avoid simply by following the process.

The model is *the* key element in making the entire ISA process work way faster than you would ever think possible. Without the model, you may get the results you're looking for, but it will cost you a tremendous amount of time and money and give you way more headaches than you'd want to experience.

This book gives you a detailed, unabridged look at exactly what the model is and how it works.

The Seven Insider Secrets You Came Here to Learn

As I mentioned previously, there are activities, behaviors, and metrics that must be tracked and monitored in order to successfully navigate the model on the way to great results. While there are thousands of factors that can affect the outcomes you seek in implementing an ISA department in your business, there are seven key areas that will have the biggest impact in creating a predictable pipeline of listing business.

All seven of them will be discussed in detail in this book. Here's a brief look at each element and the part it plays in the entire ISA process:

Hiring: 97% of the success of any relationship—personal or business— is based on the choice you make. Choosing the wrong person can have a domino effect on what happens with the rest of your ISA department. We'll show you how to get the right person on board virtually every time to avoid the nightmares associated with hiring the wrong person.

Hiring the right people helps you create predictability for both your organization and your sales department. Good employees flock to companies like Microsoft, Apple, Coke, and Frito Lay, and stay, because they simplify life for them and provide an atmosphere of consistency and growth (otherwise known as a predictable experience). When good people stay at your company, you can rely on them and their efforts to produce high-quality work and a consistent experience for your clients. When clients see this, they not only do repeat business with you, they also refer their friends and family, which means you now have a "machine" that produces consistent and predictable sales for you.

Making good choices with hires also helps you avoid the Potted-Plant Syndrome (PPS). PPS is a "disease" that affects an individual in a group of people. The disease presents itself when the person joins a group of people, but does not participate in discussions, improve the culture, or add value to his/her surroundings. The individual does nothing but take up space—like a potted plant. Good hires prevent this from happening.

Effort: Most ISAs aren't even calling and talking to enough people each day for you to reach your goals. Putting in the right amount of effort is crucial to success. In this book, you'll find out how much effort is truly needed for you to hit your goals and how effort can go way beyond how many dials your ISA makes each day.

Peter Drucker once said, "If you can't measure it, you can't improve it." This holds especially true when it comes to the effort your ISAs put forth every day. By accurately measuring the effort your ISAs exhibit each day, you are able to determine a baseline of productivity for the dials, contacts, nurtures, and appointments he/she produces daily. Having this baseline gives you the plumb line to determine if more effort is needed or not, and more specifically, where the additional effort is needed to reach your goals. It also tells you when (and when not) to spend more money on labor so that you're not throwing money away generating more leads and hiring employees when you don't need to.

Skills: Your ISA(s) should be every bit as good as you or your outside sales reps in the sales process. If an ISA doesn't know what to say, how to say it, and when to say it, he/she cannot be the main point of contact for your prospects. In this book, I'll identify what your ISA(s) need(s) to know to properly influence prospects over the phone.

The one thing you can't teach anyone is to be fearless on the phone. Other than that, every other skill you need to be successful on the phone can be learned. The important thing to remember is that your ISA needs to have all the skills at his/her disposal to be a beast on the phone. I liken it to being someone who disarms bombs: That person doesn't just want to know some of the skills necessary to disarm bombs, that person wants to know all the skills.

In mastering all the skills necessary to be a rock star on the phone, your ISA will not only be more independent in his/her daily activities, he/she will convert leads at a higher level...leading to more and better appointments and ultimately, more listings and sales.

Processes, Tools, and Systems: You wouldn't bang a nail in with a screwdriver, right? Having the right dialer, CRM, and digital delivery methods for messages can mean the difference between bad results and gargantuan results. You'll get the inside scoop on what to look for in the tools to use in order to get optimal results.

Prospects, Nurtures, Leads: Not all lead sources are created equal. Bad phone numbers, wrong names and addresses, improperly targeted neighborhoods all lead to fewer appointments, listings that are harder to sell, and higher labor and marketing costs. Having the right data can increase your ability to contact the right people by as much as 50 percent. We'll tell you what to look for when choosing the right leads and then how to handle them to supercharge your conversion.

Managing: If you're a great salesperson, you're likely not the best manager. It's a learned skill, at best, but one that's vital to getting the best results from your ISA(s). We're going to discuss key strategies on how to effectively manage your ISA without taking away from the other things you do every day.

Reporting: Reporting is like the rudder for your ship. There are numbers you need to look at every day to make sure your ISA department is delivering in spades on the investment you're making in it. We'll talk about the key metrics you must keep an eye on in order get consistent, predictable results for your business.

Now, before we get into all of that, I want to cover two things with you: 1) our philosophy of the ISA as it relates to the real estate industry, and 2) how to get the most out of this book based upon where you are in the life cycle of your ISA department.

Inside Sales vs. Outside Sales

Having an ISA represents a segmentation of duties within your organization. It takes the job of building relationships and selling over the phone out of your hands or the hands your outside sales associates (OSAs) and puts it into the hands of an equally skilled individual who actually enjoys working on the phone.

More importantly, it allows for specialization of duties, which will open the door for you to make more contacts and build better relationships with your prospects…leading to a larger number of appointments with better-qualified prospects.

Specifically, it gives you the bandwidth to sell more homes, faster and with greater ease than if you were to do it all yourself.

ISAs are highly trained, highly skilled individuals who have the same skill levels as their outside sales counterparts. They are experts at influencing over the phone and have the ability to build incredible relationships with prospects, which result in high-quality appointments with prospects that are ready to take action.

An important distinction to note here is what inside sales is not.

Inside sales is not a process where you employ a "win or go home" strategy on every phone call. That approach has its own name: telemarketing.

With telemarketing, the task at hand on every call is to make a sale. If you make a sale, great; if not, it's on to the next phone call with no thought as to what you're going to do with your last "no."

Telemarketers, as a rule, are not highly skilled and highly trained in the art of selling and influencing over the phone. Rather, they look to get down and dirty on every phone call with no regard for creating a relationship that could lead to a sale.

It's one and done on every call.

The reason I know this is because this is how I generated sales for my business when I was calling, how I trained my ISAs to make calls for me when I listed 367 homes in one year and how most of the agents in the US and Canada—likely including you—are doing it right now.

Can you make money doing it this way?

You can, but you are forever in "hunt and kill" mode and are often only a month or two away from putting your business in a financial body bag.

If the flow of expireds, withdrawns, and FSBOs come to a screeching halt or if your database of leads hasn't been cultivated properly, you're going to be hard-pressed to create consistency and predictability in your business.

Conversely, with an ISA and a proven inside sales strategy, you can generate seller lead opportunities almost every day and pack your pipeline with current and future seller opportunities no matter what the market sentiment is at the time.

What's even better is that with an inside sales department, your prospects are continually being cultivated to become more familiar with you, your systems, and what you can do for them that your competition can't.

So, when your prospects are ready to sell, you're a virtual shoo-in to get their listing.

16

Yes, there are some moving parts you'll need to learn how to use in order put yourself in the expert category when it comes to your ISA and inside sales department.

The good news is this book is going to give you some over-the-top strategies to harnessing the seven crucial elements of building and operating an inside sales department that gets you jaw-dropping results.

Which leads me to my next point: What's the best way for you to get the most out of this book?

The answer is simple—and not so simple.

You see, whether you're looking to hire an ISA or if you have an ISA and are looking to improve on or duplicate his/her results...

...you'll need to make sure you nail every aspect of your first ISA hire (and getting the department up and running like a well-oiled machine).

Once you've done that, the sky's the limit for you and your inside sales goals and dreams.

To that end, in order to squeeze all of the nectar from the fruit of your labor, read each chapter—preferably in order—and see if you've done everything the way I've suggested it needs to be done.

If you have, give yourself a pat on the back, move on to the next chapter, and do the same thing.

If you haven't, not to worry.

In addition to scores of tips and strategies throughout the book, I would love to hear from you. You can also email me directly at *michael@insidesalespredictability.com* with any question you might have in regards to nailing and/or scaling your inside sales department.

One last thought: A very good friend of mine shared a really great perspective on happiness. He says happiness is measured by the gap between where you are and where you want to be.

My goal is to help you get from where you are to where you want to be faster than you would imagine it to be possible and make you ecstatic with the results you get from your ISA.

CHAPTER 1 - HIRING

"Hire salespeople who are really smart problem solvers, but lack courage, hunger and competitiveness, and your company will go out of business."
- Ben Horowitz

I'll never forget seeing Jim Collins for the first time. It was at an Inc. 500/5000 conference; I was sitting in the front row patiently waiting to hear his talk. At the time he was the one author whose books I had consumed the most. Jim opened up his keynote with a message that was so profound, I really think it could be the best advice for business owners: "Seven out of your top 10 decisions throughout your career will be people decisions."

Mind blowing, right?

What did that mean exactly? He wasn't the first person I've ever heard talk about how significantly the right hire could impact your business. Not knowing what he meant specifically, I was left to my own interpretation. It's pretty obvious the point he was making was that hiring the right person could be the biggest fulcrum for leverage in your business.

Here's another quote from Mariah Delon, the Vice President of People for Glassdoor, one of the fastest-growing jobs and recruiting site. In it, Delon talks about the perils of hiring the wrong person.

> *"No business owner wants to hire the wrong person for a job.*
> *Not only because they'll need to find a replacement candidate*
> *sooner than they'd like but also because making a bad hire drains*
> *energy and time and can cost a business in a number of ways."*
> *– Mariah Delon, Vice President of People, Glassdoor*

If you're like most agents, the person you hired—or are looking to hire—as your ISA is someone you know. Or someone that was referred to you by someone you know. At the outset, it doesn't seem like a bad decision because in real estate, working with a referral is historically easier and better than working with someone you don't know and who doesn't know you.

Unfortunately, this is likely one of the biggest mistakes you can make as a business owner (for a number of reasons).

Because the person is "familiar" to us, we make assumptions that this hire will work harder, is better qualified, is more flexible, will be easier to manage, and in the end, will get us better results faster and easier than if we brought someone in off the street.

Nothing could be further from the truth.

Historically, all of these assumptions end up being wrong. Because the person is familiar to us, they sometimes feel that you'll take it easier on them, that they're entitled to different treatment versus other people on your team, and worst of all, that they can take liberties with their time and effort—read: take it easy and not work as hard—that other employees might not necessarily do.

How damaging to your business is it to hire the wrong person?

Let's take a look at some statistics...

In a recent survey of CEOs by Robert Half International, the world's largest accounting and staffing firm:

- 39% of the CEOs said that a bad hire cost them significant productivity.
- 11% of those surveyed said that the bad hire also cost them sales.
- The survey also said that supervisors (that's you in your business) spend 17% of their time—roughly one day per week—managing poorly performing employees.
- Lastly, the US Department of Labor estimates that the cost of a bad hire a can equal 30% of the employee's first-year earnings.

If you're a large company, this is bad news.

If you're a sole proprietor like most real estate agents are, this is news that could cripple—and even destroy—your business.

Scared yet?

Well don't be.

It's as Easy as 1, 2, 3, 4

You see, there are some simple strategies and processes you can employ to weed out the bad hires and put the right person in the ISA seat on your team. If you already have an ISA, don't worry; you can still use what I'm going to share here as a barometer for whether or not your current ISA is the right person for the job.

There are three key elements to ensuring that you make a job offer to a prospect who will knock it out of the park as the ISA on your team, and they are: the Ad, the Interview, the Onboarding process, and Training.

Let's look at each one in detail.

The Ad

Garbage in is garbage out, right? This philosophy has been around since the 19th century, but it's still as valid today as it was back then. In order to begin with a good strategy and end up with the right person, there are a few things you need to get right when creating and placing your ad.

There are many places you can run your ad to get employment prospects to reach out to you:

- www.indeed.com
- www.ziprecruiter.com
- www.careerbuilder.com
- www.wizehire.com
- www.craigslist.org

Online job ads tend to get you the best results in the shortest amount of time for the least amount of money. Be sure to use a good ad, be clear in what you're offering and make sure that your contact information is complete and detailed. A wrong number in your phone number or letter in your email address will impact your results negatively.

Right Job Description

If you want to hire the best person to occupy the ISA seat in your organization, you need to use the right words to attract the best person…

…and it all starts with the words you use in your headline.

For instance, take the word "telemarketer" or the word "telemarketing." What images do either of those words conjure in your mind?

Do you see a seasoned sales professional who builds relationships with prospects to incubate and nurture them until they are ready to sell—with you?

Or do you see a huckster who sells subscriptions to magazines or newspapers, vinyl siding you don't need for your brick-faced house,

25

a free vacation that leads to a tortuous two-hour pitch for a timeshare, discounted ED medicine from Canada, or any other of the myriad things you don't want or need to purchase over the phone?

If you saw a huckster, you're like the 100,000 other people each month who call the Attorney General, FCC, and other regulatory organizations about "harassing" telemarketing calls.

And if you saw that image, it's likely the people who see your ad's headline are having the same image pop into their heads, which means they're: 1) not going to read the ad, 2) not going to apply for the job, or 3) the kind of people you don't want as the main point of contact for prospects in your real estate organization.

Like "telemarketer," there are other words you want to avoid when writing the headline for your ISA ad. By using them, you're attracting the wrong prospects for the job and putting yourself at a disadvantage literally from the word go.

Attract the Right Person

Conversely, there are words and phrases that you will want to use in the headline and body of the ad to ensure that you catch the attention of the ideal prospect.

At the same time, there are some do's and don'ts when it comes to writing a good ad.

Here are some things to consider when writing your ad, according to Monster.com:

1. The headline and job title are the most important part of your job listing. They appear in the body of your text and search engines use it to determine what keyword phrases your job listing is relevant on.

2. Make your job title compelling, but most importantly, relevant, in order that seekers click on your job listing over others.

3. Make it simple, concise, specific. Doing so makes your ad more appealing and more likely to get read.

4. In the body of your ad, include the job type—without abbreviations—and avoid company jargon and acronyms. The easier it is for the prospect to determine what the job offer is (and the clearer your offer is) the more likely you'll get the targeted and ideal prospect you seek.

Words like "Inside Sales Representative," "Expert in Selling on the Phone," "Seasoned Phone Sales Representative" are going to get you the type of job seekers you desire. Words like "telemarketer" and "telemarketing" will not.

5. Avoid the following approaches, as they make your listings appear less professional and more like spam:
- Deceptive/inaccurate titles
- Posing questions in your titles
- Keyword "stuffing" in titles

- Including the salary or rate of pay in titles
- Capitalizing words (unless appropriate) in titles
- Mentioning "No experience required" in titles

Remember: Search engines are only concerned with text, so your job description is your best chance to have your job posting appear in search results, and the best way to do that is to integrate keyword phrases throughout your job listing.

More importantly, your higher-quality, more-suitable employment prospects will appreciate the professionalism of your job posting... which means they're more likely to click on it and be the ideal candidate that you seek.

If you're looking to be super direct and strategic in finding the right candidate, you can go to a website like LinkedIn and search specifically for prospects with actual Inside Sales experience and even for those who have a certification in conducting sales over the phone.

Right Compensation Model

There are times to be thrifty in your real estate businesses and there are times where being thrifty isn't a good choice. Your compensation or On Target Earnings (OTE) for your ISA is one of those times where being thrifty isn't a good choice.

If you remember, an ISA is a highly skilled, highly trained salesperson who is as good as an outside sales associate...but excels at (and enjoys) selling and building relationships over the phone.

In order to secure the right person for the job and keep them over the long term, you need to offer the ability for your ISA to make a solid income for himself/herself.

The national average OTE for an ISA hovers somewhere between $55K and $65K, with a portion of the compensation coming from salary and the remainder coming from bonuses or commission on homes sold. That said, it would be beneficial for you to check www.salary.com to determine where in the ISA compensation range your area falls.

From my perspective, I like what Charlie Munger has to say about compensating team members. Munger is the Vice Chairman of Berkshire Hathaway and has been Warren Buffet's right hand man for the last 56 years. He's 92, currently worth $1.29 billion, and responsible for helping Berkshire Hathaway a company that churns out billions in profits each year.

Here's what he has to say about compensation models when attracting and retaining top talent, "You also have to have a compensation system that's satisfactory.... at Berkshire Hathaway, we have no [single] system; we have different systems. They're very simple and we don't tend to revisit them very often. It's *amazing* how well it's worked."

In order to retain top talent, you need to do more than throw a number at a potential employee. To keep good people on board, you need a compensation model that provides depth and opportunity for your ISAs to earn a solid income for themselves.

A compensation model is a methodology of paying an employee that takes into consideration salary, bonuses, and incentives while helping you accomplish two things: provide your employee with a seat at the table that has significant upside, without leaving you on the hook for paying everything out of pocket, up front, to make it happen.

With a strong compensation model, you can limit your exposure on salary when you hire an ISA that underperforms. At the same time, it will help you retain the right ISA and reward him/her with serious money for a job well done.

The Power and Danger of Incentives

"Perhaps the most important rule in management is to get the incentives right." – Charlie Munger

Your compensation model will need to have incentives in order to attract and retain a world-beater for an ISA. That said, providing incentives to your employees—especially your ISAs and OSAs—can be a double-edged sword. Yes, a good incentive can get salespeople to move mountains, but it can also be abused if your salespeople don't use it properly to help you build your business to be the most profitable and efficient it can be.

Charlie Munger believes that people respond most willingly to what they see as their incentive or disincentive. Therein, he speaks of "human misjudgement" or more specifically, he wonders why we do what we do, and more importantly, why are we open to doing certain things while we abstain from doing others? The answer has a carrot-and-a-stick flavor to it, but the philosophy is not that cut and dry.

In situations where we need to come up with an appropriate incentive, Munger suggests we always ask: "What is someone getting out of this?" Asking this question helps us align our incentives with what will motivate our employees the most.

To demonstrate how vexing it can be to provide employees with proper incentives, Munger shared the following example in his *Poor Charlie's Almanack*:

- **FedEx**: The company couldn't get packages moved from plane to plane in a timely manner during the night shift. The challenge was that the workers were getting paid by the hour. There really wasn't an incentive for them to move packages at an expedited rate. When FedEx changed to paying the workers per shift, the workers were motivated to get the job done faster because once they were done moving packages, they were done working (and they would still get paid for the entire shift).
- **Xerox**: At the time, Xerox was the big boy on the block and it paid incentives to its salespeople to move certain copiers. The problem was that the incentives were heavier on the older, inferior copy machines instead of the newer, better-performing machines. Sales of the older machines were crushing those of the newer machines. Company founder, Joe Wilson, who had already left Xerox, came back to resolve the problem by changing the incentive structure to favor the sales of the newer machines.

Through these examples, it's easy to see not only the power of incentives, but also how they can be dangerous when not handled properly. To handle them properly, we must do first what Munger suggests: Ask what our people will get out of doing what we ask of them.

In short, all of our "radios" are tuned to our favorite radio station, WIIFM (What's In It For Me). And with that as our internal driver, we usually do what we can to increase the pleasure we feel, while at the same time avoiding or reducing pain. In virtually any situation, we look at the carrot and the stick and act in a way that meets our needs in the best way possible. Knowing this, we need to provide incentives for our ISAs— and all our employees—that provides them with the impetus they need to perform at a high level while delivering what we need to the bottom line.

This is the only strategy that will provide a huge win-win for both you and your ISA.

Breaking Down the Incentives

The location, quality, and source of your leads will dictate how you incentivize your ISA.

For instance, when a prospect calls you—an inbound call—because of your marketing and advertising efforts (radio, television, postcards, home evaluation leads, etc.) that lead will likely convert more easily. As a result of that, you're going to pay your ISA a smaller incentive when the listing sells. Additionally, the lead costs more, so you'll also pay a smaller incentive on incoming calls because you'll want to recoup your investment.

On the other hand, expireds, withdrawns, FSBOs, demand generation, and in certain cases, home evaluation leads—leads for which you make an outbound call—cost you less money to generate, but will require more work and diligence from your ISA. With these leads, your incentive for the ISA to help procure sales will be higher.

As well, if you have an ISA already, you can consider hiring a Sales Development Representative (SDR) to assist your ISA in identifying future seller opportunities, otherwise known as nurtures. Nurtures will be discussed in detail later in the book, but for now, just know that a nurture is a seller who wants to sell in the next year and is willing to let you stay in touch with him/her and is open to working with you down the road. Nurtures have a fairly high conversion rate and will become some of your best listing appointments, listings, and sales on a month-over-month basis.

If you do hire an SDR to cultivate listing opportunities, you'll want to give him/her a small incentive for each nurture that he/she uncovers and then give your ISA a smaller incentive when he/she converts the nurture to a listing sale. By doing this, you can compensate two employees to generate more listing opportunities without screwing up your compensation and financial models to do so. Your cost of sale goes up by doing this, but you can balance it out by offering smaller, but competitive, incentives to your SDR and ISA.

ISA vs. SDR

An SDR performs a Demand Generation role. Demand generation is the focus of targeted marketing and calling efforts to drive familiarity and awareness of an organization's products and/or services. This form of lead generation is the lowest customer acquisition cost (CAC) and here's why:

Historically, an SDR's skills are not as deeply developed as an ISAs and they don't need to be. To that end, you can pay them less money. On a daily basis, an SDR is going to be calling into targeted areas and unearthing opportunities for both now business and more importantly, nurtures. The cost of doing demand generation to acquire a customer is much lower because it's nothing more than what you pay your SDR. There are no marketing costs as it's the SDR's job to find the opportunities for you from the data you provide to them and introduce your company and its services to the prospects personally.

ISAs are also going to be making outbound calls, but they are also going to be handling inbound opportunities as well. If your ISA is amazing on the phone and converts your inbound opportunities at a high rate, your CAC can remain lower. That said, if he/she isn't as effective, you're going to be paying more for marketing and labor and experience a much higher CAC.

Your ultimate goal is to have a low CAC from both your ISAs and SDRs and hire them based upon their skill sets to do each specific job at its highest level.

All of this said, your salary needs to be enough to ensure your ISA can eat, pay bills, and afford gas to get back and forth from work. The bonuses and incentives need to be enough for your ISA to want to bust his/her hump to earn the other side of their compensation…and maybe even more.

Getting the right person for the job starts with a great headline, and the right job advertisement and ends with a solid compensation package that offers a competitive OTE.

Hiring Funnel

It's safe to say that you don't want to interview every person who submits a resume for the ISA position at your office. Much like real estate sales, you want to sit in front of ready, willing, and able candidates that are a perfect fit for your team. In order to sift and sort through the pretenders to get to the contenders, there are some things you can do with a hiring funnel to make sure that only the best and brightest interview for the job.

Finding Applicants

Your ad goes at the top of the funnel and it should produce a decent number of applicants for you to choose from for an initial interview. The ad should give candidates the opportunity to click through to a lead capture page where they can answer a few qualifying questions. In addition to the questions, you may want them to call a recorded line and leave a message for a prospective seller to hear how they sound on the phone. One of the questions should be: "Tell us why you think you're a great candidate for the job."

Personality Profile

Include a link to a DISC test for them to take. You're looking for a high D and I (or a high I and D) personality. The high D indicates a prospect with a task orientation who is willing to ask the hard questions, overcome call reluctance (if there is any), and to get to three to four responses of "no" before he/she gives up—if he/she gives up at all. The high I reveals a prospect who can build rapport with anyone in virtually any situation. A person with a high I is a natural conversationalist who can carry on a conversation and put people at ease, even when the person is not known to him/her ahead of time. Not having a high D and I is not necessarily a deal breaker, but it's highly recommended when moving your prospect to the next stage of the process.

Here's a quick overview of all four "ideal" personality types:

High D: Moderate to strong focus on tasks and goals; known for achieving results through people; prefers team leadership structure

High I: Energized by people and opportunities to motivate and persuade; confident and outgoing

Low S: Strong sense of urgency; motivated by activity, variety, and change

Low C: Independent; creative thinker with limited interest in details or logistics

Again, the personality profile is not the be-all-and-end-all determinant in selecting your ISA... but it needs to play a huge part in your decision-making process.

Group Interview

Start the process with a group interview that gives you an inside look at whether this person would be a good fit with your organization. The group interview should be a measuring stick to see if the candidates match up well with your core values.

Your company's core values are the guiding principles that provide a framework for acceptable practices, attitudes, and actions from employees. They assist your employees in determining right from wrong and they give you a barometer if your employees are helping you achieve your business goals. Most importantly, they provide a constant reference for acceptable behavior within your organization.

This is likely one the most critical parts of the hiring process because no matter how amazing an ISA prospect is on the phone, if he/she is going to blow up your business' culture and be reviled by the rest of your employees, there's no benefit to having this person on your staff. Your goal in the group interview is to ask great questions related to your core values to determine how good of a fit your candidates are.

At the end of the group interview, you'll have a clear idea of who would be a great addition to your team. Most importantly, you won't be wasting your time with someone who isn't.

To ensure that they want you as much as you want them, you'll have all candidates who are interested in a one-on-one interview send an email to your office saying, "I'm a team player," in the subject line. This mutual consent allows for a great platform to conduct the in-person interview; no arm twisting, cajoling, begging, or any other over-the-top influencing will need to happen. You want them and they want you.

One-on-One Interview

If you remember nothing else from this section of the book, please remember this: Do not—and I repeat—do not hire or even bring someone in for an interview that doesn't have any prior phone sales experience.

I've tested this strategy for you, in detail, so you don't have to make the same mistakes I made.

Whether you're hiring your first ISA or you have one and you're looking for another one, 10, or 100, you are not looking to take a flyer on someone. Your goal is to find someone who has a solid skill set for working with prospects over the phone—whether they were strictly an Inside Sales Representative or they were a salesperson who set all of their own appointments and managed their own pipeline. Bringing someone other than that type of prospect in through your door for an interview is likely going to lead to you sending them out that very same door in the next 60 to 90 days.

It's just not worth it.

That said, let's take a look at what makes for a good interview and what you need to say and do to find an ISA that can deliver the goods.

Ask Good Questions

When someone sits in front of you, there are three things you're looking for: Can they do the job, will they do the job, and are they a good team fit? The best candidates will be a resounding "Yes" and are likely going to be wickedly effective on the phone for you.

To ferret out the answers you need in determining the best fit, you need to ask good questions of the person sitting in front of you.

Now, there's always some small talk in an interview where you ask some basic questions about the candidate to get the ball rolling. Questions like: "What did you like about your last job?," "What do you like about inside sales?," "Are you okay with being on the phone all day?," "What do you want to be when you grow up?," etc.

These questions are helpful in getting to know your candidate, but they're not the type of questions you need to get answered in order to make a solid decision for your business.

The questions you need to ask get to the bottom of how this person is wired...how they'll handle the job of being an ISA on a day-over-day basis.

Some of those questions are:

- "What's your stance on objections, how do you feel about them?"
- "How do you feel about rejection?"
- "What do you do when you've been rejected by someone over the phone or face to face?"
- "What's the best sale you've ever made?"
- "How many "No's" do you need to get before you give up?"
- "What's your strategy when you can't get in contact with someone?"
- "How do you feel about scripts and dialogues?"
- "What's your definition of rapport and how do you build it over the phone?"

Asking questions like these will give you a legitimate gauge as to whether or not this person can do the job that is being asked of them and if they're willing to do the job you're wanting and needing them to do.

Role-Play to Dig Deeper

One of the best ways to determine if an ISA candidate is going to kill it on the phone is to see him/her in action by doing a role-play or two with them.

I usually lead into the role-play by asking them about the toughest objection they faced in any of their prior inside sales or sales jobs. By doing this, I'm setting them up to give me their best shot at dealing with the objection that may have stopped them in their tracks in the past.

Once they tell me what it is, I say, "Great. Let's go ahead and role-play that." I put them on the spot and see how they not only handle the objection, but also how they deal with pressure.

You may see some red faces, sweaty palms, and dry mouths, but the badass ISA candidates are going to eat that role-play for lunch and handle it as well as you would—with master's-level savvy.

For the rest of the candidates who aren't the right person for the job, that role-play session is going to eat their lunch, effectively weeding them out of the process.

In addition to seeing how they perform in the heat of battle, you're also looking to hear their tone of voice during the process. People's tone of voice conveys virtually everything about them: their confidence, what's going on in their mind at the time, and how emotionally grounded they are. It also reveals how resilient, empathetic, ambitious, and open they are.

Resilience is the ability to cope with and transcend adverse reality. It is the ability to work through disappointments, failures, misfortunes, suffering without collapsing. It enables a person over time to transcend pain, suffering, disappointment, and failures. ISAs are frequently confronted by disappointment. It's their resilience and ability to turn the disappointment around that makes them effective.

Empathy is the ability to comprehend precisely the emotional and psychological state of other people, including their desires and motives.

Through empathy...*you understand and share another person's experiences and emotions.*

Ambition is the most important of the four talents. Ambition is the drive to be successful in every sense of the word. Ambition is the continuous pursuit of excellence in every vital and meaningful undertaking in one's life. Ambition is bigger than just being competitive. It's wider than achievement in our job. Ambition refers to the intensity with which one pursues happiness. ISAs must be ambitious in order to succeed in their position.

Openness refers to curiosity about the world in which we find ourselves. It is the desire to learn new things and to acquaint oneself with new ideas. Openness refers to a tolerance for different points of view, to an appreciation of the differences and richness in life. A person with robust openness seeks to expand his/her beliefs about one's social environment, science, culture, hobbies...anything of significance to a person. It's the desire to learn information about everything and anything.

Resilience, empathy, ambition, and openness are key attributes of top ISAs and you don't want to hire an ISA that lacks in any of these areas.

What you should find is that candidates with a high D personality will reveal a tremendous amount of resilience and ambition in their role-plays and interviews with you. People with high D personalities are often pioneering and not afraid to push forward in reaching their goals.

At the same time, candidates with high I personalities are likely to exhibit a high degree of empathy and openness. High I ISAs are willing to carry on conversation with just about anyone and to a certain extent, care what others think about them. To that end, they are more willing to get along with their prospects through empathy and being open to what they hear and encounter on the phone. These traits are critical to being an amazing ISA and a candidate with a high I should fit the part well.

A good interview with good questions will ensure that you don't miss the mark.

At this point, people often ask me: "What happens if the candidate is a superstar on the phone, but isn't a core value fit?" My answer is simple: "Don't hire them."

And here's why...

According to the same survey from Robert Half International that I mentioned earlier, 95 percent of financial executives surveyed said that making a bad hire at least somewhat affects the morale of the team, and 35 percent said a poor hire greatly influences employee morale. In many cases, bad hires do not get along with other employees, which can cause additional problems for the cohesiveness of your team.

Unfortunately, sometimes we get excited about a candidate and we overlook the core value fit simply to put a "check in the box" regarding the hire. It's vital to hire someone who can do the job, will do the job, and who is ultimately a good team fit in order to get the best results you can from the ISA.

Once you've decided that a candidate is the best person for the job, there are some things you'll need to review with him/her before you have him/her sign their contract.

Compensation

Since the job is part salary and part commission, the candidate needs to know that he/she isn't likely to earn commission on a sale for 90 to 120 days due to the life cycle of a converted listing lead in real estate. From there, each month the compensation will increase as his/her pipeline fills with opportunities that become listings and then sales.

In the end, though, he/she needs to be okay with—and be able to live on—the salary that you are paying them. If that can't happen, you have a tough decision to make, because hiring someone who is in a tight financial spot can lead to:

1. Having them set marginal appointments for you with the hope the home will get listed and sold so they can make money fast
2. You hiring someone only to have them leave in a couple of months because they need more money, or
3. having an employee who isn't focused on the job at hand because he/she is worried more about their personal finances than doing his/her best job

You want no part of these scenarios, and if it's even close, it's best not to take the chance as *you* will be the one who is likely left holding the bag. To get a better idea of what a great compensation model for your company, go to www.insidesalespredictability.com/compensation to get a copy of our compensation table and model breakdown.

Expectations Prior to Their First Day

You want your ISA to hit the ground running his/her first day on the job. To ensure that he/she is in position to do that, you'll want to give him/her the scripts and dialogues he/she will be using on a day-to-day basis.

The goal is to have the ISA take the scripts home, handwrite each one, practice all of them and learn what to say before his/her first day. Will the scripts be perfect? No. But the ISA will have internalized enough for you to role-play with him/her on his/her first day and get on the phone 24 to 48 hours later.

Usually, a week is a long enough time for the ISA to get familiar with your scripts. For an ISA with a strong inside sales and/or sales background, it could take even less time. The last ISA we just hired did it in a weekend, so it can happen pretty quickly.

Also, give the ISA a couple of books to read before they come in. We recommend *Question Based Selling* by Thomas Freese and *Go for No* by Andrea Waltz and Richard Fenton. Both books are great for people who sell on the phone and they really speak to the mindset we're looking for from our ISAs as they attend to their daily activities. They also provide some great strategies for asking good questions over the phone and on how to advance a sales call.

I would get both of them to your ISA and have him/her read them both before his/her first day on the job. If you'd like to download the interview I did with Waltz and Fenton for free, go to www.insidesalespredictability.com/gofornointerview

Once you have the contract signed, give the assignment for your scripts and hand over both books, pick a start date (a week or less later), and have the ISA commit to getting everything done and being prepared to rock and roll on the first day.

When it comes to picking a candidate, remember what Tony Robbins says: "Ninety-seven percent of the success in any relationship—business or personal—is the choice you make." Do your due diligence and interview wisely, and you'll end up with a blue chipper for an ISA.

Welcome Aboard

Will Rogers said it best: "You never get a second chance to make a first impression." Nothing could be truer than when it comes to bringing a new person on to your team.

If you're like I am, you want your ISA—or anyone who joins your team—to walk through the door of your office on their first day and feel like they came to the right place to work, to a place where they can take care of their family and put themselves in a position to be wildly successful.

The best way to do this is to make sure you have a well-defined onboarding strategy through which you can take your ISA during his/

her first couple of months on the job. And by well-defined, I mean that the entire process has been laid out ahead of time and that there is an actual checklist that your ISA can see with his/her own eyes, which can be followed, step-by-step, to help put them in position to succeed sooner.

In addition to putting your ISA in position to know what it's going to take to master the position, it gives you the ability to guide them, as needed, when they hit sticking points. Ultimately, it provides you and them with clear guidelines for success and failure, especially in the event that you need to let them go.

Here's what our onboarding process looks like.

Expectations Meeting

The first thing we do when an ISA joins our team is to have an expectations meeting with them. In this meeting, our expectations of them and what they're supposed to accomplish on a daily basis are clearly laid out.

As part of this meeting, we let them know:

- The hours they will work each day
- Their schedule, including calls, breaks, and role-play sessions
- How many dials, contacts, nurtures, and appointments are required of them daily
- What scripts they need to internalize
- What their goals are for the first month they are with us
- What their goals are for each month thereafter

- What success and failure look like
- What will happen after 30 to 60 days if they don't reach their goals

By having this meeting, you and the ISA know where each person stands, the ISA knows what questions he/she needs to ask if things aren't clear and what will happen if he/she doesn't succeed at the job. And, while the goal is to help your ISA become wildly successful, everyone needs to be on the same page from day one regarding what will happen if success is not achieved.

It's important to mention here that the benchmark dates that you mention in the expectations meeting are scheduled in the calendar on the person's first day on the job. That way, you and your new ISA can see clearly that the expectations are firm and that there will be discussions around these expectations at specific points in the future.

Running the Show

In order to ensure that the onboarding process is going to be taken seriously by a new ISA, we have assigned the responsibility of taking him/her through it to someone on our staff.

This person reviews the entire process—which is highlighted by our 84-day onboarding checklist—and then holds the ISA accountable to getting each activity completed on each of the 84 days. By doing this, we know the the ISA will learn what they need to learn and build the habits necessary to be in the position to start setting appointments within his/her first couple of days on the phone.

If you'd like a free copy of our 84-day onboarding checklist help get your ISA(s) onboarded so that they start performing at a high level from day one, go to www.insidesalespredictability.com/onboarding and grab it for yourself.

Training

Your ISA's greatest asset is being able to know what to say, how to say it, and when to say it. In Chapter 3, we'll be talking about the actual skills your ISA will need to possess to hit things dead solid perfect on the phone call after call. There you'll find out in eye-popping detail exactly what your ISA needs to do and say to get solid listing appointments day after day after day.

For the purpose of this chapter, however, we're going to discuss what it takes to get your ISA in position to work magic on the phone for you. In it, we'll discuss how you—the best salesperson in your organization— can teach your ISA to replicate your skill set on the phone quickly and effectively by using a time-tested, but under-utilized strategy.

Everybody and their brother knows about it...but only the successful agents use it.

Sharpening Their Axe

Abraham Lincoln was credited with the following saying: "If I had six hours to chop down a tree, I'd spend five hours sharpening my axe."

In order to get good results, fast, you'll need to help your ISA sharpen his/her axe with training in two major areas: training on processes, systems, operations, and technology and then training over time on their skills.

Let's look at each one separately.

Processes, Systems, Operations, and Technology

At our office, we have a number of processes and systems we use to run our business, as well as some internal operations and technology to make the job of selling homes easier.

Each ISA is trained on how to do their job and understand what role they play in making the machine run as it pertains to the processes, systems, operations, and technology that apply to them. The training in all four of these areas happens for a short period of time during the 84-day onboarding period, usually at the beginning of their tenure with our company. The goal is to get them to be as autonomous as possible as quickly as possible so they can focus more on doing what we need them to do—set appointments.

There's nothing sexy about this part of our training, but it's vital to the success of our organization. If an ISA can't get their head around how to disposition a lead, hand an appointment off to a listing partner, manage their prospects in the CRM, or navigate the dialer, he/she will never be effective enough to make a difference in your organization. This training is vital to the your success and that of your ISA—never shortcut this part of the training process.

Skills

You know what to say, how to say it, and when to say it. Being able to do that got you to where you are in your business today.

Now that you're not going to be making calls as often (if at all), your ISA needs to be as good as (if not better than) you with all the skills necessary to build relationships, move prospects along in their pipeline, and set appointments consistently. These skills range from scripts and dialogues to influencing prospects over the phone, from active listening to being an expert at asking questions, from handling objections to using tie downs, trial closes and closes to gain commitments from prospects...and everything in between.

This type of training never ends. You will continually work on all aspects of selling over the phone with your ISAs. You'll do this by:

- Holding weekly training sessions
- Role-playing with your ISA (or getting them a role-play partner)
- Shadowing him/her on live calls and giving him/her feedback
- Reviewing recorded calls with him/her and breaking the call down
- Having your ISA handwrite the script every couple of days until they internalize it

There's no shortage of things you can do to train your ISA on improving his/her skill set. The most important thing is that you never stop training your ISA as long as they work for you.

Your reward will be a larger number of high-quality appointments.

I Do It, We Do It, You Do It

The easiest and fastest way to transfer your knowledge and skills to your ISA is through a strategy called "I do it, we do it, you do it." The methodology has been around for hundreds of years as it has been used by tribes to transfer knowledge, skill sets, and traditions down from one generation to another.

With this approach, your ISA gets to see the perfect model (you) in action, receives the proper instruction with your involvement and isn't left alone on an island trying to figure things out by himself/herself with little guidance from you.

Here's how it works:

I do it: You will make calls and your ISA will sit and listen as you prospect the various types of seller leads you work in your business. When doing this, you'll point out important points for your ISA to make note of and help your ISA learn by watching you.

We do it: You and your ISA sit together for prospecting sessions. In these sessions, you and your ISA alternate back and forth in making calls. You give the ISA feedback on ways to improve and you also make note of better ways to handle certain situations based on how you handle your calls.

You do it: You will sit with your ISA and let him/her make all the calls. As he/she makes the calls, you will give feedback and help make your ISA as independent as possible on the phone before you turn the reins over to them completely.

Unfortunately, many real estate agents want so badly to get an ISA in place and stop making prospecting calls that they skip this hands-on approach and often throw their ISAs to the wolves too early. This can be a huge mistake because it will take your ISA a lot longer to become successful on the phone. As well, bad habits can form and you may not get the lights-out results you're looking for.

Very important: Just because you hired an ISA does not mean you can stop making prospecting calls altogether. You must gradually work your way out of the job of prospecting and the "I do it, we do it, you do it" approach is the perfect way to make that happen.

Overall, the hiring process is fraught with all kinds of pitfalls and challenges that can derail your inside sales efforts...even before your ISA makes his/her first call. By following the process we've laid out for you in this chapter, you should have a good handle on where all the bodies are buried to get optimal results from your ISA department.

Make sure your hiring ad is on point and relevant so you attract the best candidates. Make sure you do a thorough job of vetting your prospects so you hire the absolute best candidate possible. Don't skip the onboarding process. In fact, make sure it's laid out ahead of time and very detailed.

Remember, you can get a copy of our 84-day onboarding checklist by going to www.insidesalespredictability.com/onboarding

Lastly, train, train, train so you know your ISA can do the job lock, stock, and barrel.

CHAPTER 2 - EFFORT

"The achievements of an organization are the results of the combined effort of each individual."
- Vince Lombardi, Head Coach Green Bay Packers, 1959 - 1967

If you did your job based upon what I shared in Chapter 1, you hired an ISA who makes putting forth effort seem effortless. More specifically, you hired someone who is self-driven and motivated and who sees putting forth effort as nothing more than doing what comes naturally to them because they're driven to succeed.

There's no doubt that you want an ambitious ISA who has an actively engaged mojo, giving them the foundation to put forth consistent and focused effort. It's a huge component to your ISA's success and a requirement that can't be overlooked when building your inside sales department.

You know you need it, but what is effort, exactly, as it pertains to an ISA? And, once you identify the types of effort he/she can put forth, how do you measure it and then improve upon it when it's not up to par?

These are all important questions to which you need the answers, and I'm going to tackle each one of them separately in this chapter.

What Is Effort?

I remember how much effort I put forth in getting my business up and running: the hours of prospecting, the number of times I called the same prospects and going three, four, and sometimes five "NO's" deep to get an appointment. Effort was the hallmark of my success, so it was the place I focused most when I first implemented inside sales in my business.

Simply defined, effort is someone's ability to overcome resistance. And the more comfortable your ISA is with being able to do this, the better the results will be.

For an ISA, the main resistance he/she must overcome in his/her job is that of making phone calls.

If it's not obvious, please allow me to make it obvious: Call reluctance of any kind is a huge deal breaker when hiring an ISA. A person cannot and will not put forth the necessary effort (no matter how much money you are paying him/her) if he/she has call reluctance. It's safe to say that you should never hire anyone who feels any resistance whatsoever to picking up the phone and making calls.

Now, that's not to say an ISA doesn't hit a slump every once in a while or need a break from the phones here and there...I'm simply saying that a great ISA candidate has no call reluctance and will put in the effort necessary to reach the daily, weekly, monthly, and annual goals you set forth.

How Much Effort is Needed?

Having coached a number of agents, I'm fairly confident when I say that believe many agents in today's market don't know how much effort actually goes into producing a solid listing appointment. I don't say this so much from the standpoint that they don't work hard. Rather, I'm saying it from the perspective that they don't know specifically how much effort needs to be put forth, from a numerical perspective, to get great results, especially when calling a lead source that is not a personal or agent-to-agent referral.

To shed some light on what those numbers look like, I want to share the results of a study that real estate industry news giant, Inman, conducted a few years back to determine the effectiveness of cold calling as a baseline activity for lead generation.

The numbers were very telling:

Agents in 10 geographic areas completed 14 hours of lead generation over 14 days. It was conducted by agents who had "no experience, no contacts, no database, no marketing, no listings, and no 'just-solds'[...]"

- 6,264 calls were made: 1,037 we bad numbers and 3,450 did not answer. Overall, 71.6 percent of all calls failed to reach a live person.

- For the 28.4 percent where contact was made with a live person, 929 (14.8 percent) said they had no interest; 132 (2.1 percent) of those contacted requested a call back.
- During the calling period, the agents set 19 appointments and received 11 referrals. Specifically, it took 208 calls to get an appointment or referral.

There was a 1.7 percent conversion ratio for agents when they actually reached a person, meaning for every 60 people the agent reached, the agent would either receive a referral or schedule an appointment.

Here's what Inman determined through this study:

1. By making 50 calls per hour, it will take an agent roughly six hours to set a single appointment.
2. It was gleaned from the results gathered in this study that the listing ratio was 2-1, which means for every 12 hours of calls, an agent can expect to actually list one home.
3. Based upon an average commission of $4,641, that equals an hourly rate of $386.75.

Now, although this data takes into consideration an extremely "cold" calling environment, it really shows you how much effort actually has to go into making calls for an agent to get an appointment and then a listing.

Now that you know, my hope is that you'll better understand the value of having (or getting better results from) an ISA.

Effort Doesn't Stop There

As you look at the daily activities of an ISA, you'll see that there are a number of places where effort is mandatory for him/her to get strong, consistent results in the front-line trenches. The predictability you want and need in your business all starts with the effort put forth by your ISAs and the activities they complete on a daily basis.

Here are some of the many areas where solid effort makes a huge difference:

- **KPIs/Leading Indicators**: A leading indicator is a measurable factor that can impact, and even help predict, a specific result.

  Key Performance Indicators (KPIs) are activities help you to determine the things that you need to do on a daily basis. They give you benchmarks on how would you measure yourself for success, on how you get to your goal.

  For instance, say you wanted to get in better shape and started going to the gym. Your weekly KPIs would be: total days gone to the gym, total number exercises you do, total number of reps you do, total number of minutes of cardio you do.

  By tracking these on a daily, weekly, monthly, annual basis, you can look back and see what led to the results you obtained and also if anything needed to be changed to get better results.

In the world of real estate sales, there are a number of KPIs that lead to the end result—a home sold—and they all take real, consistent, unmitigated effort to get the job done.

- **Dials**: There needs to be a requisite number of dials each day to ensure contact with enough prospects to create nurtures and appointments that can turn into listings. It's important to realize that we're not just looking for dials, we're looking for legitimate dials to prospects who are likely sellers within the next year.

- **Contacts**: Sales is a contact sport, right? The more good prospects you contact, the better chance you have of setting legitimate listing appointments. Your goal should be to contact between nine and 12 percent of your calling list each day. The hit rate will be heavily dependent on the quality of the list and the time of day/week that you are calling. Simply by improving our contact rate from 38 to 42 percent, we were able to see a measurable jump in nurtures and appointments.

To take your contacts to an even higher level, you'll want to implement a predictable contact formula that automates follow-up with your prospects. By adding planned texts and emails to your call sequence, you can dramatically increase the number of prospects that call, text, and email you back. Our automated system helped us set nine listing appointments the first week we had it in place. Predictability is the name of the game with your ISA department, and having an automated contact strategy in place adds a tremendous amount of value to creating a predictable pipeline of listing opportunities.

- **Nurtures**: These are a Key Result Indicator (KRI). By making a certain number of dials and contacts, the result will be a specific number of nurtures. A KRI will tell you if your KPI(s) are not only the right benchmarks, but also if the volume of each KPI is sufficient enough to get the results you want.

  This KRI takes more skill than the first two KPIs. A nurture is a prospect that is going to sell in the upcoming 12 months, who is not committed to another agent and is willing to let you stay in touch with them until he/she is ready to sell. A nurture will sometimes require multiple calls to convert them to an appointment. As you can imagine, nurtures aren't always forthright with their plans when being prospected, so a good ISA needs to know how to ask the right questions and more importantly, to read between the lines to determine if this seller merits additional calls in the future.

  Lastly, with our targets for nurtures at 3.5 per day and appointments at 1, you can see how much more likely it is you'll get a nurture on the phone in one day than you could get a one-call close for a listing appointment. It's because of this level of availability (and the ensuing ease in building a relationship from a nurture) that makes nurtures so attractive.

- **Appointments**: This is where the rubber meets the road...so to speak. If your ISA has made enough quality dials and contacts, and if he/she has done a good job with nurtures, appointments should come as a natural, predictable, and consistent conclusion. The number of appointments you get are elastic to the three KPIs I just reviewed.

It's vital to remember that the "garbage in, garbage out" philosophy applies here, too. Weak lead sources, poor effort with dials and poor nurture identification and selection skills can lead to not only a limited number of appointments, but also low-quality appointments, too.

An important effort to make note of when setting appointments—in addition to mastering the proper skills to actually set them—is going after objections and "No's" like a crazed bulldog. Statistically speaking, you have a 66 percent chance of getting a "Yes" if you're willing to work through four "No's." Your ISA must put in the effort to work through all roadblocks to seal the deal on appointments.

Take note: Properly nurtured leads move 23 days faster and sell for nine percent more money than leads that are converted at the initial point of contact.

- **Follow-up**: Jim Rohn said it best: "There are pennies in a sale, but there's a fortune in the follow-up." Statistically speaking, only three percent of your prospects are now sellers or buyers and only another 20 percent are looking to move within the next 90 days. That means the majority of prospects are going to require some sort of consistent follow-up in order to be converted from suspects to prospects and prospects to clients. It's one of the precursors to incredible conversion. There is major effort required in the follow-up department to create the predictability that top inside sales departments exhibit.

- **Dream 100 Management**: Your ISA could never stay in touch with every person in your database consistently, and quite honestly you wouldn't want him/her to do so. That said, I'm a huge fan of Chet Holmes and his strategies on following up with prospects. As a result my affinity for his teachings, I've adopted his "Dream 100" approach for our ISA department.

When it comes to staying in touch with prospects, Holmes once said: "Follow-up makes the difference between mediocrity and greatness." This holds especially true when it comes to dealing with the cream of the crop in your prospect database—your Dream 100.

The goal is to put forth the effort to identify 100 sellers who meet the criteria of a nurture and then maintain an ongoing relationship through calls, texts, and emails.

The real effort gets exerted in topgrading this pipeline on a daily basis. Each day, as a seller in your ISA's Dream 100 shows up as an opportunity to call in the CRM for a potential listing appointment, your ISA must contact the seller and 1) set an appointment, 2) move the seller prospect to another date for future follow-up, or 3) remove the seller prospect from the list and replace him/her with another, better opportunity.

Mastering this strategy and putting forth the right amount of effort is crucial to capturing the largest share of listing opportunities you can. Letting follow-up dates go by and/or not calling nurtures in his/her Dream 100 list can lead to a lot of waste and missed selling opportunities.

- **Notes in Your CRM**: In order to mine the gold in your database, you need to know where it is located and how to extract it when you find it. Your ISA needs to gather good information about seller prospects and record it in the form of notes in your CRM. The notes should be detailed enough for anyone who looks at them to make reasonable assumptions about the timing, motivation, and overall situation of the prospect, but not so detailed that it takes forever to read them.

  In addition to gathering data for an initial set of notes, your ISA needs to put forth additional effort to get more information prospects each time he/she talks with them. The process is called "progressive profiling" and it's the act of discovering new and different information from prospects that can be used to strengthen relationships, build even more rapport with and have the ability to influence them at a higher level in order to get them to agree to meeting with you to list their home. Great notes are the foundation to properly working leads in your database.

- **Role-Play**: Your ISA's currency on the phone is their ability to handle any situation that comes up with professionalism and ease. The only way that he/she is going to get good enough to effectively replace you and get you the predictable results you want and deserve is to become outrageously good with scripts and dialogues, which will only happen with regular review and practice of them via role-plays. All ISAs should put forth the effort to role-play for at least 30 minutes per day, Monday through Friday, until they've mastered each script and dialogue and how to use them at a ridiculously high level. Then, when they've become an expert, they can teach others through role-playing to maintain a high level of mastery with the words that they say each and every day.

To make role-play sessions effective, you'll want to mix things up a little bit so that your ISA's sensory acuity improves with each session. For instance, do some role-plays face to face and then do them back to back where the ISA can't use body language to his/her advantage. As well, do some role-plays over the phone where the ISA has to call you directly. Make some noise, don't pay attention and make your ISA work to control the call. Be sure to switch up scripts and scenarios as often as possible and absolutely be tough on your ISA during role-plays. The tougher you are on him/her in practice, the better he/she will perform at game time.

- **Follow Processes/Don't Cut Corners**: The effort required here applies to all the aforementioned elements of putting forth effort. Taking shortcuts, not following procedures and ignoring processes that have been created expressly to ensure success is a sure trip to your ISA getting shown the door. Sometimes people get lazy or they think they know a better way to do something and it's counter-productive in every way. A good ISA will make the effort to follow your instructions and do things the way you've laid them out for the ISA. It starts with you picking the ISA as a good core value fit and ends with him/her doing things as prescribed to knock the ball out of the park every day.

Effort is important, but it's not enough. You need to give your ISA feedback on a consistent basis to ensure that his/her effort is being refined and channeled regularly to continually improve his/her results. We use this amazing one-on-one meeting sheet to give our ISAs feedback on their activities and results each week. You can get a copy for yourself at www.insidesalespredictability.com/one-on-one.

Pulling Out the Measuring Stick

Anything that can be measured can be improved. For your ISA to make consistent improvements and be a cog in the machine that provides you with predictable results in your listing business, he/she is going to need feedback on where the holes are in his/her game.

The best way to do that is to set benchmarks for your ISA, hold him/her accountable to those benchmarks and then give feedback on how to make improvements when he/she falls short as quickly and efficiently as you can.

Setting Benchmarks

"It is not enough to do your best; you must know what to do, and then do your best." - W. Edwards Deming

W. Edwards Deming was, among other things, an engineer and an incredible management consultant. Credited as the father of the post-World War II economic miracle in Japan, Deming was steadfast in his commitment to continuous improvement as strategy for helping companies meet and exceed their goals. He was amazing at identifying benchmarks, reviewing the results from these benchmarks and then making adjustments to them in order to create incremental and lasting improvements.

As the leader of your business, it's vital to set your benchmarks in order to help you hit your goals and create long-term success.

As I mentioned earlier, in order to get enough dials and contacts each day, your ISA needs an ample number of leads with good phone numbers. The number of dials you're looking for per day is in a range between 450 and 550 outbound dials. From there, you're looking for at least 35 to 45 contacts from that set of dials.

If you hit those two benchmarks, you should be able to get between 2.5 and 3.5 nurtures and one appointment per day...the other two benchmarks you're looking to hit each day. These benchmarks, or milestones, are part of the bigger picture you must design for yourself in the form of a personal economic model.

With a personal economic model, you always start with the end in mind and then reverse engineer your strategy to get you there in the form of benchmarks and bite-sized pieces. It's an approach that's served me well in my business and it's one that we use with our partners in helping them become the go-to agent in their market service area (MSA).

The model starts with doing the math, i.e., determining and understanding your personal leading indicators and then establishing conversion benchmarks across the spectrum so that you can actually know exactly what you need to do in order to accomplish your goal.

More specifically, we identify how much money we want to make and from there, we look at how many dials, contacts, nurtures, and appointments are needed on a daily basis based upon their conversion rate at the kitchen table to help us reach that number.

We covered the KPIs and benchmarks, in detail, in the prior section. Setting them is the easy part—hitting them is going to take a little more work. To hit them requires a little planning and math, then a lot of elbow grease.

Daily Accountability

Our ISAs submit a report to the members of our leadership team at the end of each day. This Daily Accountability Report is emailed to the members of our leadership team and it includes the results of their calling efforts for the day. In addition to providing the details of their dials, contacts, nurtures, and appointments, they also record the names and addresses of each nurture and appointment they scored for the day.

The Daily Accountability Report is reviewed by the Sales Director. It's his job to monitor the ISAs' daily results and make sure that each ISA is on point for reaching their benchmarks. He observes the results on a day-over-day basis and reviews them each morning in the ISA team huddle.

In the morning huddle, the ISAs announce their results from the prior day in front of the group so they can own their results and be pushed by those of the other ISAs. The huddle acts a format for the ISAs to not only bond as a group, but also to hold each other accountable (and encourage each other when someone is having a tough stretch). From our perspective, there are five main benefits of this daily accountability strategy:

1. **Accountability accelerates performance**. Having to stand up and talk about their performance from the prior day pushes the ISAs to show up and work hard each day to get better results.

2. **Accountability helps measure success and progress**. The benchmarks are established, the daily huddle gives everyone a barometer of what their results are and how close they are to meeting and/or exceeding the standards that have been set.

3. **Accountability keeps people involved**. Things come up to get us off our game all the time. Personal life, boredom, fear, getting distracted, feeling tired...they can all get us off course. Having to show up and be accountable for their results each day keeps our ISAs involved in the process of their success.

4. **Accountability keeps people responsible**. Accepting responsibility for our actions and results keeps us in line and motivated to do better day in and day out. By having to account for their actions, our ISAs must take a close look at themselves and begin to eliminate excuses while taking specific actions to get the results they and we want them to achieve.

5. **Accountability validates beliefs**. When we're held accountable by someone, we can bounce thoughts and ideas off of them to either

confirm or disqualify what we believe, helping us get better clarity about our goals and what we have to do to achieve them.

In the end, dials, contacts, nurtures, and appointments drive the train toward helping our ISAs reach their goals while helping our OSAs reach theirs.

Another Layer of Accountability

Getting regular appointments for our OSAs is great—don't get me wrong—but if the appointments aren't with sellers who are ready, willing, and able to sell, they're not worth our OSA's time. In fact, we tell our ISAs to ask themselves if they would spend time away from their family, invest their own money in gas to drive to the appointment and get dressed up to go on each of the appointments they set. If their answer is "No," then we tell them not to send the OSA either.

One of the ways we gauge if an ISA is setting good appointments is to add another a layer of accountability by looking at the percentage of listing appointments they set that actually turn into listings taken. If an ISA sets appointments and they turn into listings taken on a consistent basis, then they are good. If the opposite is happening and listings aren't getting taken, we get to work on helping them improve their phone game.

Making Improvements

Your goal as a team leader is to not let too much time pass if your ISA is not getting the results that you're expecting of him/her. If he/she is not hitting benchmarks or is setting appointments that aren't turning into listings, you must take corrective measures as soon as you see the problems. Otherwise, bad habits will continue to form and worst of all, time and money will be wasted and eventually lost.

There are three main things you can do to rectify problems that your ISA is having on the phone:

- **Role-Play**: Perfect practice makes perfect. If your ISA needs more than 30 minutes of role-play each day, find him/her multiple role-play partners to help with sharpening skills on scripts and dialogues. You can't practice this part of the inside sales game enough, especially for an ISA whose results are lagging.

- **Shadow your ISA**: This is the "we do it" portion of the training strategy I discussed earlier. Make time to sit with your ISA and monitor his/her calls live. The great part about this approach is that you can give immediate feedback when he/she makes a mistake, which allows for the lesson to set in and be worked on and implemented in real time.

- **Review recorded calls**: One of the best teachers for anyone who works in sales is the sound of their own voice. When we listen to a recording of our own voice, we can hear things we say and how we say them in a way we would never be able to do in the "heat of the battle." Many times, we can pick up a mistake in a matter of seconds simply by listening with an open mind.

In addition to that, recordings help you and your ISA zero in on strategic questions such as:

- What common questions are being asked?
- Which objections are regularly being used?
- How are ISAs successfully handling objections and overcoming obstacles?

In the end, your ISA needs to expend effort that is strong, consistent, and full of intent if he/she is going to reach their goals and help you and your OSAs reach theirs. The effort required for creating predictable results varies by task, process, and system and it's up to you to guide your ISA and hold him/her accountable to keep the effort and results coming consistently. You, as a leader, need to take an active role in your ISA's accountability, education, and growth. Failing to do so will have catastrophic results and send you back to square one to hire another ISA. Effort and consistency are the name of the game.

CHAPTER 3 - SKILLS

"Knowledge is not skill.
Knowledge plus ten thousand times is skill."
- Shinichi Suzuki,
Violinist, inventor of the international
Suzuki method of music education

Confidence on the phone comes from being highly skilled in what to say, how to say it, and when to say it. When you're cool as ice on the phone and there's nothing that a prospect can say to get you off your game...all bets are off as to how far you can go.

The great news about skills is that they can be learned. If you learned them, then your ISA can learn them. And, you mastered them, you can teach them to your ISA and shorten their learning curve dramatically.

Now, in order for you to create an enterprise that provides consistent and predictable listings and sales, skills mastery is an absolute must for every ISA (and OSA) on your team. Let's take a look at three building blocks necessary to help you collect your unfair share of the business in your marketplace.

What to Say

According to Master Sales Trainer, Eric Lofholm:

"Why do powerful scripts work? Powerful scripts work because human beings respond in predictable ways.

Here is one of the first scripts I learned: "If you do what a millionaire does you will get what a millionaire has. If you invest your money where millionaires currently have their money invested, what will you become?"

I have asked this question of over 1,000 people. Every single one of them has always answered "a millionaire." Isn't that powerful?

If you didn't fully grasp the power of the example above let me restate my point. You can create PREDICTABILITY in your sales presentation. That is what the sales superstars do. They use the same scripts over and over again because they [create predictability] and work."

I think that about says it all. Say the right thing every time, control the dialogue between the prospect, and you and you can create predictability that kills. Here are a few things to consider when it comes to saying the right things.

Provide Features and Benefits

During the Great Depression, Elmer Wheeler was known as America's #1 Salesperson. He was credited with a number of successful sales phrases including one virtually every salesperson knows today: "Sell the sizzle, not the steak." Wheeler's recommendation is a wise one as it's benefits—not features—that get salespeople the leverage to move people from prospects to consumers.

Unfortunately, most real estate agents focus on the features instead of the benefits and that's where they lose sales. Many agents talk about being number one, their 88-point listing system, access to all the listings on the MLS and how honorable they are…

…when they should really be focusing on how all these features make their clients money, save them time and reduce the headaches and stress associated with selling a home.

Here's a brief story to illustrate how benefits-laden selling gets the best results.

A store decided it would sell bait and it put a sign out that said: "For Sale: Bait." Needless to say, the bait didn't sell at a particularly great clip. The next day, they added the word "FRESH Bait for sale" and sales picked up, but not that much.

The next day, they changed the sign to say: "For Sale: Bait known to catch the biggest fish." Again, sales picked up, but they still weren't where the store owners wanted them to be.

The next day, they put up yet another sign that said: "For Sale: Bait known to catch the biggest fish by a champion fisherman." Sales continued to pick up and on the next day, they sold out of bait using this sign: "For Sale: Bait known to catch the biggest fish by a champion fisherman: name of his favorite fishing hole and map provided."

As the benefits increased, the sales increased.

By missing the mark, agents are also missing out on opportunities to build their business and make more money themselves.

Your ISAs need to take the approach of sharing features and benefits over the phone in order to be successful. It's not enough that they sing your praises and speak chapter and verse about everything you offer, they must close the loop and help sellers understand how what you do benefits them. To get a deconstructed copy of our FSBO script, go to www.insidesalespredictability.com/fsboscript

Use Their Name

"Using a person's name is crucial, especially when meeting those we don't see very often. Respect and acceptance stem from simple acts such as remembering a person's name and using it whenever appropriate." - Dale Carnegie

Your ISA, in order to cement the rapport being built between him/her and the prospect, needs to be sure to use the prospect's name when appropriate. Dale Carnegie once said: "A person's name is the sweetest sound in the world" to them. By properly using the prospect's name in the right parts of a sales call, your ISA can really get the prospect to be far more responsive and willing to do what the ISA is asking him/her to do.

It's important that your ISA doesn't overuse the seller's name because it can be distracting and work against him/her in the effort of building rapport on the way to setting an appointment. Also, your ISA shouldn't just say the name to say the name. Your ISA should use it to make points, "Can you see, Bob, how this service will make you more money?," ask for the order, "Great, Mary, what's better for you - week-days or weekends?" and to say thank you, "Steve, it was great speaking with you today. We look forward to seeing you Saturday at 4:00 p.m."

These aren't the only places your ISA would use the prospect's name, but they are effective spots where your ISA can build rapport and strengthen his/her chances in getting a listing appointment.

Timing and Motivation

The most important pieces of information you can gather from a prospect are related to their timing and motivation. Yes, you need to know a lot of other things about your prospect, but timing and motivation trump everything. In fact, if we had to pick one characteristic that trumped everything, it would be motivation.

Why, you ask?

Motivation is more important than anything because a motivated person will run through brick walls to make things happen. Motivated sellers will do the things you ask them to do to prepare their home for sale: They'll price the their home properly to get it sold according to your recommendation and they'll work with you if you need anything done to make the sale happen.

Timing is very important, too, because many agents waste a lot of time trying to get a seller's listing way before the seller is even ready to list. The fact of the matter is that you can do just as good a job nurturing the seller with a solid text, email, direct-mail, and phone strategy, as you would by going and meeting the seller for a listing appointment way before it's time.

The sweet spot for a listing appointment is within 90 days of the seller wanting to sell (120 if there is a coming-soon opportunity with a bit of work needing to be done on the house). Timing is also crucial because if you show up too early, you may not be able get back in the door for the listing appointment, and if you show up too late, you're out of luck.

The timing doesn't have to be perfect, but it should be pretty close.

It's your ISA's job to properly identify timing and motivation in order to help you get predictable sales results. Knowing how to do this well means the difference between them keeping their job and you letting them go. And since most sellers aren't going to serve up on a silver platter the specific details of their move, your ISA is going to need to be an expert at extracting this data.

The best way to do this is to simply ask good questions.

Natural Curiosity

Great salespeople have a "Spidey-sense" that tingles when a prospect sends a nugget of useful information their way. When that happens, they pounce on the opportunity and ask information-gathering questions that will lead them to the natural conclusion they seek—a sale.

The same thing goes for ISAs.

ISAs need to be able to hear what's being said "behind" what's being said to get enough information to decide whether or not to set an appointment for you. The only way to do this is to listen very carefully to what the seller prospect is saying and then ask lots of good questions. The better the questions and the deeper your ISA goes, the better the quality of the appointment they get you (or do not get you because it doesn't make sense to set it).

Some people are naturally curious, which gives them a leg up when it comes to being a top-notch ISA. The reason is because they have a gift that allows them to ask questions from a position of unconscious competence, without having to think about what questions to ask as they navigate their way through a sales call.

Other folks aren't wired that way, but it doesn't mean that they can't master the skill of asking good questions to obtain the same result. Here are a few tips your ISA can use improve his/her natural curiosity, which will enhance his/her information-gathering skills when speaking with seller prospects:

• **Calm Your Inner Guide**. It's the voice that keeps on talking to you when listening to someone speak, and it often favors your opinion over that of the person speaking. The bad news is that we often listen to that voice instead of processing what is really being said. That voice prevents you from listening with an open mind and can often make you unable to hear the full intent of what's being said. Your job is to focus more on the person speaking and less on your inner voice.

- **Fight the Good Fight**. If you're unable to quiet that voice down, do your best to make it your friend. As soon as your opinion starts to creep in, make a concerted effort to fight the urge to let it happen and instead, hear what's being said. In the end, you're looking to find out where you're wrong and where the speaker is right. Worst-case scenario is that you'll now be open to getting other people's opinions.

- **Fake it Till You Make It**. If you can't be curious, at least act like you are. There are some advantages to being a naturally curious person. When you listen to people speak, take notes to remember what is being said. At the same time, write down questions that you could ask the speaker to enhance your curiosity. This will allow you to learn more and to show the speaker you are listening and actively involved in the conversation.

- **Seek Nuggets of Truth**. Every thought and idea has a beginning point and to that end, even the craziest of things someone might say may have a nugget of truth to it. So, even if you have trouble swallowing the whole story, be a detective and look for what may be true in what's being said. Your deductive reasoning will certainly improve and you may even be able to give the speaker feedback to improve his/her original idea.

- **Don't Ignore the Messenger**. Sometimes, we disregard what someone says because of who they are. Unfortunately, doing this can be detrimental to the learning process—especially if the person talking has some great information to share. The same can go for when we're talking with someone we know really well. Oftentimes history and familiarity with someone can skew what we listen to and give credit to. Do your best to remove the messenger from the message so you can listen objectively.

Again, whether you're naturally curious or not, you can arouse natural curiosity within yourself using these five strategies. Curiosity adds a tremendous amount of depth to every prospecting call and gives you an upper hand on your competition who are simply looking to get a sale.

It's Closing Time

One of my favorite sayings is this: "If you don't A-S-K, you don't G-E-T." In the world of setting appointments over the phone, your ISA must be able to control the conversation and direct it toward a natural end: closing for an appointment. As part of directing the process over the phone, your ISA will likely need to employ trial closes, tie downs, and gaining agreements along the way so that asking for the appointment is as natural as it can be. To see a blog post we did about nailing the close go to www.insidesalespredictability.com/nailingtheclose

Closing at the appropriate time(s) and using the appropriate verbiage is a must on a good sales call and fortunately, it is a skill that can be learned. Here are some tips your ISA can use to make sure they can thrive in the "deep end of the pool" when talking with prospects:

- **Gaining commitments**: According to sales training group The Sales Board, 62 percent of salespeople fail to ask for a commitment when making a sale or setting up an appointment. This can be devastating when you consider how much money, time, and energy a real estate agent/business owner invests into even just one sale. Neither you nor your ISA can afford to navigate a sales call or presentation without gaining commitments along the way. You can gain commitments by asking for the order (cutting to the chase only after you have rapport), summarizing the benefits of your offer, offering options or choices, and/or offering special features. The strategy you use will be predicated on your relationship with the seller prospect and what feels natural at the time based upon his/her goals.

- **Tie downs**: When you confuse your prospects, you often lose them. And when you've lost them, it's hard to get them back. Keeping your prospects on board and making sure they stay on board can be done easily by using tie downs. Tie downs are small questions that you use to confirm that your prospect got your point and agrees with it. Essentially, they are used to help you create and then maintain "Yes" momentum during your presentation over the phone or face to face.

  For example: "If you're going to get top dollar for your home, it makes sense to hire an agent who sells his clients' homes for 100 percent of asking price, doesn't it?" "Doesn't it" is the tie down here and it elicits the "Yes" you're looking for to keep the seller prospect on your side. Like any tactic or strategy you use in your sales presentations or calls, using too many tie downs can become annoying and off-putting. Try to use them sparingly and only when they make sense.

- **Trial closes**: A trial close is a smaller, less-threatening close that lets you know whether or not the prospect is ready for you to close. Trial closes are like gaining commitments in that you would use them to put yourself in position to close for an appointment or a sale. The difference, though, is that trial closes are formulated as questions.

For example, let's say you are looking to buy a smartphone. The sales-person greets you, finds out what kind of phone you're looking for and then takes you through a demo of all the bells and whistles the phone has to offer. At one point during the demo, she finds out you love to download music and points out how fast the processor is in getting music onto your phone. When she's done showing you this feature, she asks a simple question: "What do you think about the speed of the processor on this phone?" That's a simple, but effective, trial close. She's not asking you to buy the phone, she's just checking in to see if you like one of its features.

Properly executed, these softer closes will put your ISA in position to close in a natural (and not pushy) manner to get you a legitimate listing appointment. And, while there are many ways to close effectively for an appointment, we like this one because it's all encompassing and ensures that your prospect knows why you're coming to see them:

When would be a good time for [name] to come take a look at your home and provide you with the value of your home? While [name] is there, he can tell you what to do, and more importantly, what not to do to get the most amount of money for your home. At the same time, he can go over the fees and expenses to getting your home sold so you know exactly what you'll walk away with at closing.

It's simple, straightforward, and most importantly, it lets your seller prospects know that you can do everything for them that they would want as a result of a visit from a real estate agent. Now, it doesn't guarantee that you'll show up and the seller will drop to their knees and beg you to list their home. What it does do, though, is put you in the best position to provide the seller with the information they need to decide if you're the agent for the job.

Knowing this, you need to make sure your ISA uses this script every time he/she sets an appointment for you. Every single time.

How to Say It

Now that you know what your ISA needs to say, it's important that you can give him/her direction on how to say it in order to get optimal results on calls to set appointments.

Influencing someone over the phone is a lot harder than influencing someone when you are sitting face to face with them. When you meet someone, in person, you have four seconds to make a favorable impression with them. Yes, four seconds isn't a lot of time, but it's significantly longer than the ¼ of a second you have to accomplish the same result over the phone.

You see, when you're sitting with your prospects, you can see their body language, breathing pattern, what they're doing with their eyes, if they're sweating or not, etc., and you can use to your advantage the signals you're getting as you work your way through your time with them at their home. As they shift their body and eyes, change their breathing, and make movements in front of you, you can respond in kind and literally gain instant rapport with them.

Over the phone, your ISA has none of that feedback available in order to build rapport with seller prospects. As such, he/she needs to master how to influence prospects using tone of voice, pauses and stresses on words, talking fast and slow, non-verbal sounds, and even his/her own physiology when appropriate.

Here's a quick look at each of those strategies:

- **Tone of voice**: Tone of voice is the number-one influencing tool we have when talking with prospects over the phone. From the time we are infants, we start identifying the difference in tones from sounds and our interpretations of what they mean. By the time we're adults, we have very specific and discriminating meanings for tones of voice and our response to them is immediate. Tone is driven by speed and pitch. Speed is the pace at which we speak. Pitch refers to how high or how low the note of a sound is.

    - Monotone: A monotone voice conveys that you are bored.
    - Drawn-out but high-pitched voice: The voice quality means "*I don't believe what I'm hearing*" as well as panic.

- High-pitched voice: This sound means *"I'm enthusiastic."*
- Slow and low pitch: This voice quality means *"I want to be left alone."*
- Abrupt pitch: This one communicates *"I'm angry and not open to discussion."*

Your ISA's goal is to sound enthusiastic and excited to talk, but also not be too high-pitched at the same time. Also, your ISA needs to be cognisant of what he/she is hearing from people on the other end of the phone. Not only is it a great way to identify what challenges he/she may be facing during a sales call, but it gives him/her a great place to start so he/she can pace and lead the prospect to his/her tone, speed, pitch, and energy level.

- **Ways of talking**:

  - **Pauses and stresses on words**: Pauses and stresses on words are amazing non-verbal ele ments of speech that your ISA can use to effectively influence seller prospects over the phone. Your ISA can literally change the meaning of the same sentence simply by changing the stresses he/she puts on different words. For instance, simply by stressing each word differently in this sentence: "You don't want to sell now," your ISA can elicit different meanings—and even the real meaning—behind what the seller is saying about not wanting to sell. This is something you should practice with him/her on a regular basis so they can dig deeper on calls to get the information necessary to set awesome appointments for you.

Pauses are equally effective. Pauses allow your ISA to highlight your words, giving the person on the other end of the phone clues as to when one idea ends and a new one begins. This keeps your ISA from losing the prospect during the sales call. Pauses also help convey emotion because they help the ISA look authentic in the eyes of the seller prospect. They also help with building credibility because they keep your prospect engaged and they replace words like "um" and "ah." Lastly, they control the pace of the conversation, which helps your ISA maintain full control of the entire sales process over the phone.

- **Talking fast or slow**: Many salespeople are regarded as fast talkers; whether it's true or not, that's the perception. In general, it's important for your ISA to speak neither too slow, nor too fast on calls. Speaking too slowly could lead to the prospect getting bored and frustrated. Conversely, speaking too quickly could cause the prospect to mishear what's being said and get lost altogether. When on the phone, it's imperative that your ISA becomes a chameleon with respect to the pace used when speaking to people. It takes 10–30 seconds for a listener to adjust to a new voice. Therefore, it's especially important for ISAs to keep their pace fairly moderate and friendly at the outset of each new connection with a prospect. Once they've set the pace, ISAs can apply a rapport-building strategy called pacing and leading. Pacing and leading is the process of starting a conversation with someone at their pace and then slowly and gradually bringing it to your pace: fast to slow, slow to fast, or any other pace.

- **Physiology**: There is a way for your ISA to utilize physiology on the phone to influence seller prospects and even build rapport. As you know, it's easy to tell when someone is smiling, frowning, slumping in his/her chair, excited over the phone. You can tell this because of the tone of voice that's being emitted at the time. If your ISA is smiling, the seller prospect will be able to hear that. If your ISA is in a bad mood and frowning, the seller prospect will hear that. If your ISA is standing, in a good mood and using his/her body to send positive, enthusiastic energy...the seller prospect will hear that. The fact of the matter is this: Your ISA's physiology can and will impact how he/she will be perceived over the phone and therefore, it is up to him/her (and you) to make sure he/she is standing, in an empowering state, as often as possible, when on the phone. This will ensure that your ISA puts themselves in the best position to influence prospects effectively on the phone and get better-quality appointments on a day-over-day basis.

When to Say It

Once you know what to say and how to say it, it's crucial that you know when to say it in order to complete the cycle for setting consistent, good-quality appointments. Timing—as with most things in life— is important, but what's more important is listening to what seller prospects have to say so you know when to say what you need to say. That can be accomplished through a solid active listening strategy.

Active Listening

We listen all day long—every day—and as a result of that, you'd think that we would actually be decent at it. Fact is, the majority of us aren't so good at it. Research shows that we retain between 25 percent and 50 percent of what we hear—and that's on a good day. That means when your ISAs talk to a seller prospect on the phone for 10 minutes, they're paying attention to less than half of the what the prospect is saying.

Pretty horrible if you ask me.

Active listening is paying attention to the content of what's being said, to the other person's *intent* and the unspoken *emotions* that are expressed. It's listening for what's *not* being said (the meanings behind the words). *How* a person conveys what he/she is saying can tell you as much as *what* they say.

In the end, my belief is that by and large, people are honest. I don't believe it's the intention of most people to lie. That said, I do believe that when people are talking to a salesperson, their defenses go up and as a result of that, they may not be willing to be as forthright as we need them to be in order for us to help them accomplish their goals.

In essence, we need to engage in asking good questions and then active listening to hear the things that they are not saying to us. It allows for better communication for the ISA and the prospect. And it allows for much better fact-finding for the ISA so they can fill the needs and wants of the prospect.

Here are a few key concepts to keep in mind as part of a strong active listening strategy:

1. In the words of the late Steven Covey: *"Seek first to understand, then be understood."* Hear what the other person is saying before you offer your side of things.
2. You can't talk and speak: You can't talk and listen at the same time.
3. Pay attention to the other person: Be genuinely interested and show it.
4. Shut out any outside distractions: You have to be genuinely "engaged" in a conversation to encourage others to speak freely.
5. Share the prospect's brain: They have problems, needs, and opinions that are important.
6. Put yourself in their shoes: Sit tight. Don't jump to conclusions too soon. Ask yourself: "What would I be thinking and feeling if I were in their shoes??"
7. Listen for the abstract, not just words: You want to get the whole picture, not just spotty information.
8. Interject from time to time: An occasional "I see," or "uh uh," or "Is that so?" shows the other person you're still paying attention. Some is good, but too much is overkill.
9. Check your worries at the door: Your worries and problems are not connected with their situation and can impede your ability to listen to them. Take notes so you remember what's important.
10. Prepare in advance: Know what you're going to say before you get on the phone.
11. Ask reflective questions: If you're unclear, check in with the seller and ask questions that help you understand more clearly.

12. Listen for the other person's particular language and communication style: Use words and phrases that your prospect is using to connect with them at a higher level. Be sure not to mimic or imitate them—be genuine. Language patterns will always present themselves if you listen carefully.

Wrapping It Up

Now that you have an appointment in hand, it's time to make sure the appointment is worthy of the investment of your time, energy, and money. The best way to do this is through a completed Seller Counseling Interview (SCI).

An SCI is a detailed set of questions your ISA is going to ask of every seller with whom they set an appointment. The questions are geared toward the following:

* Confirming the seller's timing and motivation
* Securing details about the seller's house for pricing purposes
* Determining what, if any, competition for the seller's listing is present
* Finalizing the decision as to whether or not the listing appointment is worth keeping

Your ISA must ask—and get answers to—all the questions on the SCI and provide you with a completed one for each appointment that is set for you. Unless you have one in hand after a call, it's not a true appointment.

You may be asking, "Am I jeopardizing the appointment by asking so many questions after setting it?" The answer is unequivocally "NO!"

Time is your most valuable resource and spending three to four hours of your time planning for, driving to and from, and sitting in an appointment that will lead to nothing is a huge waste of time. A properly completed SCI will help you do everything you can to prevent this colossal waste of your time and resources.

Going on an appointment without a completed SCI is akin to driving to the butcher, getting your favorite steak, cooking it on an open grill and then throwing it in the trash without taking a bite—a complete waste.

Everything I covered in this chapter can be learned and mastered by anyone who is committed to the task. As the leader of your organization, you must master these skills so that you can support your ISA when he/she is being onboarded and trained. The better job you do of teaching your ISA what to say, how to say it, and when to say it, the sooner you can do two things: 1) replace yourself in the inside sales department, and 2) create a predictable stream of listing appointments to help grow your business faster than you could ever imagine.

CHAPTER 4 - PROCESSES, TOOLS, AND SYSTEMS

*"Consistent alignment of capabilities and internal pro-
cesses with the customer value proposition is the core
of any strategy execution."*
- Robert S. Kaplan,
Emeritus Professor, Harvard Business School

All successful organizations are like trains: They run on a track and they complete what they set out to do on time. The only way they can make this happen is by creating processes and systems and having the right tools at their disposal.

The processes and systems are documented, in detail, so that anyone who comes in fresh off the street can start doing their job well simply by following what's been laid out for them. All three elements of a successful enterprise are heavily vetted, tested, and are proven to work before they are accepted as the way to do things within the organization. Doing things in this way provides a reliable platform on which predictable revenue streams can be built.

Processes

According to Business Process Management software expert, Appian:

> *"[A]...process is a collection of linked tasks which find their end in the delivery of a service or product to a client. A...process has also been defined as a set of activities and tasks that, once completed, will accomplish an organizational goal. The process must involve clearly defined inputs and a single output. These inputs are made up of all of the factors which contribute (either directly or indirectly) to the added value of a service or product."*

Processes are a vital component of any successful company, and having seamless processes in place guarantee that your business will run smoothly with or without you. Your goal as a business owner should be to have your real estate enterprise be process dependent and not people dependent. A benefit of achieving this outcome—in addition to having a well-oiled machine in place—is that you can add and subtract staff members, as necessary, and not experience a huge gap in efficiency or service during the the transition.

Leads that are not followed up on and/or poorly followed up on are the largest source of bleeding in most real estate companies. By implementing a few key processes in your inside sales department, you can ensure that you get the ROI you want and deserve from your investment in not only lead generation, but also in your ISA and the tools he/she uses to convert them.

Process Audit

The process management gurus at Transition Support—David Hoyle and John Thompson—define a process audit as:

"[A]n examination of results to determine whether the activities, resources and behaviors that cause them are being managed efficiently and effectively. A process audit is not simply following a trail through a department from input to output—this is a transaction audit. Processes generate results therefore for an audit to be a process audit it has to establish whether the results are being generated by an effectively managed process."

As the leader of your company, you should perform process audits on all of your company's processes every quarter at a minimum. Performing these audits ensure that your processes are most robust and effective that they can be while continuing to get you the results you seek. Failing to audit your processes could lead to a huge lag in results (and it will make it harder to fix any problems that come up along the way).

As well, it's important to take any processes that you've created on pieces of paper or notecards and create them digitally. Doing this will allow you to record them where they won't get lost and it gives you the ability to make changes and audit your processes more easily.

Life Cycle of a Lead

The first and likely most important process you need to nail down is what happens to a lead from the time it shows up in your database until the time that lead buys or sells a home from you or someone else. As with all processes, it needs to be detailed in a process chart and followed exactly as prescribed. The process needs to include, but not be limited to:

- What is the source of the lead?
- Where does the lead start its life cycle?
- Who calls the lead?
- When does the lead need to be called?
- When should you follow up?
- How often should you follow up?
- What script is used when the lead is called?
- What are the possible dispositions of the lead, i.e., no answer, lost, bad number, follow up, nurture, market watch?
- What happens with each of those disposition elements, i.e., set follow-up call, send notecard and magnetic business card, set nurture next-action date?
- Whose responsibility is each disposition element and action?
- Which reminders need to be sent and to whom they are going?
- What texts and emails need to be sent based on the disposition element?
- What happens when an appointment is set?
- Which agent gets the appointment?
- What happens if the seller prospect reschedules or cancels?
- What happens if the agent gets the listing?
- What happens if the agent doesn't get the listing?
- Who follows up when the agent doesn't get the listing?

This is just a sample of some of the pieces that fit into the process for handling the life cycle of a lead. The more detailed the process, the easier it is to follow, and the better job it does in keeping from falling through the cracks.

The result is a streamlined, step-by-step plan that provides for a high level of accountability for everyone involved. It also provides for higher lead conversion and ultimately better and predictable profits.

Chain of Custody

Orphaned leads mean lost money; so in order to make sure that you know precisely what happens with each lead (and not lose truckloads of hard-earned commissions) it's important that you have a chain of custody for each lead.

A chain of custody for your leads lets your ISA—and the other folks in your company—know what happens with a lead from the moment it hits your radar screen and more importantly, who's responsible for what part of the lead conversion process. Additionally, it prescribes a specific action plan/step at each stage of the process to ensure that the lead is handled properly and gets the redirected as necessary based upon the next action step in the process.

You should create your own chain of custody based upon what happens to a lead at your office. It should include the lead generation portal from which it originates, where it goes in your CRM, who has first crack at the lead, what happens to the lead if there is or is not an appointment set, how the lead is handed off from the ISA to the agent, etc. The more clear you are on the chain, the easier it is to find out where any breakdowns occur.

It may seem like a tedious task, but creating a proper chain of custody for your leads can save you thousands of dollars every year in lost opportunities.

Dispositions

The word disposition is just another word for outcome, especially as it applies to calls made from an inside sales person. Every call that's made by your ISA has an outcome and every outcome needs to be recorded in your CRM in order to optimize your sales team's sales progress.

In addition to providing clarity in purpose and direction for your ISAs and OSAs so they can do their jobs better each day, dispositioning leads also gives you, the rainmaker, clues as to why certain trends may or may not be occurring in your business.

Most importantly, call dispositioning saves a bunch of time, giving your ISA a one-click shortcut for call outcomes, saving him/her from additional note taking where it's not necessary. When in the middle of an outbound dialer session, consider how dispositioning makes life easier for your ISA when tracking the results on 500 dials: Did you reach the right person? Do I need to follow up again? Was it the wrong or busy number? In each instance, your ISA can click a button and have many of the details they need recorded for them with the original call record and not lose much calling time.

Here are the disposition categories we currently use:

- **No Answer**: The number was called and no contact was made. This disposition category does not speak to the validity of the number called, it just notates that the number was called and it wasn't answered.

- **Bad Number**: A bad number disposition means that you called the number and the wrong person answered, it was the wrong address, you heard a disconnected phone notice, or got a fax number.

- **Lost**: With this disposition, we spoke with the right person, but for some reason, they or we choose not to do business with that person right now. The contact may not be moving at all, have a relative/friend in the business to whom they are committed, be hard to understand over the phone, etc. Just because the lead is not one that you can convert now, doesn't mean that you may not want to try to convert it at a future date. In that case, you would make it a follow-up.

- **Follow Up**: In this case, you called the right person and it may or may not be the right time for them to move. Your ISA would use this disposition to set a call date in the future with a seller prospect that he/she believes will make a move in the future.

Follow-ups historically are done manually and with the deliberate of intentions to convert your prospect into a listing appointment. A follow-up call can result in:

- An appointment
- A future follow-up call
- A decision to discontinue following up with a lead
- A lost opportunity
- A referral

No matter the outcome, it's important for follow-ups to happen consistently and be dispositioned properly as part of a proper lead management process.

- **Nurture**: The nurture disposition requires a set number of criteria to be met. The seller prospect must be looking to move in the next year, have good contact information for future contact, be open to working with you and to hearing from you in the future regarding helping with selling his/her home.

- **Market Watch**: A market watch disposition is used when you speak with the right person and he/she isn't quite ready to sell but may be considering it at a time in the distant future. With this disposition, the seller will receive a branded market report for his/her area every month until you stop sending it or they request you to stop sending it.

- **Scheduled Appointment**: This disposition is only used when an appointment has been set and scheduled (with a time and date) and a seller counseling interview has been completed in detail. Absent that, it's not a valid appointment.

Dispositioning leads properly is the only way to effectively keep track of which opportunities your ISA is going to work and the ones on which he/she shouldn't spend any time. More importantly, it provides a coding system for collecting data and creating reports that help you determine what changes need to be made to create predictable pipelines of opportunities in your business.

The Handoff

The handoff of an appointment from the ISA to the listing agent starts as an extension of the main process for the life cycle of a lead...and then transitions to another, separate process that goes from the handoff to the actual listing appointment.

Having a solid process for the handoff is crucial because the handoff sets the tenor for the entire listing process. If the ISA has done a good job building a relationship with the seller prospect, nailed the timing and motivation, collected great data on the seller prospect, and successfully completed the seller counseling interview, the handoff should go extremely well.

As part of the handoff, the ISA sets an appointment in the listing agent's calendar and then provides him/her with a completed seller counseling interview. In addition to that, the ISA takes detailed notes in the CRM about the seller prospect so that the agent has as much information as he/she needs to be prepared for the listing appointment.

Also, if there are any mitigating circumstances, i.e., seller is unrealistic about sales price, there is a divorce situation, house needs a lot of work, etc., surrounding the seller's situation, the ISA will set up a quick call with the listing agent to ensure that he/she is aware of the details prior to walking through the front door.

Once the appointment is set and qualified, the ISA sends out our whiteboard video via email to the seller so that the seller can familiarize himself/herself with our selling system. After that the ISA makes sure that our listing tear sheet and white paper (authority builders)—as well as our list of testimonials—are sent to the seller so that he/she is well versed on our partner and what we do to help him/her reach all of their goals better than any other agent in the area.

The combination of all these efforts puts the listing agent in the best position to succeed at getting the listing. To that end, the more clear and detailed the ISA is on every aspect of the appointment-setting process, the better the handoff is. And the better the handoff is, the more quality listing appointments you get and take.

In the end, the predictability you want and need from your ISA department is largely dependent on the job the ISA does to set and then hand off the appointment to the listing agent. Having the ISA shadow several listing appointments to learn what happens at the kitchen table, in addition to following the correct process every time, makes successful listing appointments a legitimate reality.

It's that simple.

Fortune Is in the Follow-Up

If you recall from Chapter 2, only three percent of the prospects with whom you speak are ready to pull the trigger on making a move right now...the rest of them are 90 days or more out from moving. Knowing this, it shouldn't come as a surprise that even after your ISA follows the appointment-setting and handoff process to the letter and sets what he/she believes to be an ironclad listing appointment, some people still won't be ready to/want to list when the listing agent comes to the house. They may be a week away, a month away, or longer. So when this happens—and it's going to happen—you need to have a process to make sure that the opportunity doesn't slip through the cracks.

You see, once your ISA is making calls and following the processes you've laid out for him/her, he/she is going to do a great job in setting appointments for you. In some cases, he/she is going to do such a good job that he/she will get you into sellers' houses for listing appointments, sometimes earlier than the sellers are ready to sell (even though the seller said he/she was ready at the time the appointment was set).

Consequently, you or your listing partner will have gone on an appointment, built a relationship with the seller, and left the house without listing paperwork signed. The good news is that you will have a legitimate opportunity to get that listing in the future, but it's going to require some consistent follow-up.

The process for following up when you don't get the listing is simple:

1. Have your ISA write and then send a thank you note, with brownies, to the seller thanking him/her for spending time with you. Most agents won't even send a thank you note, so this package should help you stand out.

    As an example, our ISAs write this in their note cards:

    > Dear [First Name],
    > Thank you for your time today! I look forward to talking again in a couple of [weeks]. In the meantime, if you need expert advice related to real estate, here is [Agent's] contact info.
    > All the best,
    > [ISA First Name]

    (And then they enclose the agent's business card magnet, hand address and stamp the envelope, and mail it that day)

2. If the potential listing date is less than 30 days out, the listing agent usually handles the follow-up process with the seller until the day comes that the home is ready to be listed.

3. If the potential listing date is more than 30 days out, the listing agent turns the follow-up process back over to the ISA who will remain in contact with the seller until the day comes that the home is ready to be listed.

There are two schools of thought when it comes to this part of the lead management process. The first is letting the ISA maintain contact with the seller for the entire process—before and after the listing appointment—when a home isn't listed. The benefit of doing it this way ensures that the opportunity doesn't fall through the cracks after the listing appointment.

The challenge with this strategy is that the listing agent has spent hours with the prospect and might have a better relationship with the prospect at this point.

The second is letting the agent own the relationship. In addition to having a tremendous amount of rapport with the seller, the listing agent has a great feel for the seller's wants and needs and is more likely to able to be in the right place at the right time.

On the negative side, listing agents get busy and often, follow up is not their strong suit. There is a possibility that the opportunity will be lost because of this potential issue.

No matter which side you choose, this process absolutely must be in place and followed properly with each listing opportunity that is not captured at the kitchen table. Out of sight is very often out of mind when it comes to sellers and real estate agents, and you'll certainly lose out on all your and your ISA's hard work if you don't follow up properly and consistently when you don't get the listing at the first visit.

Lastly, you'll want to have regular meetings scheduled between your listing partners and your ISA to track the results of all past appointments and review the pipeline of nurtures, future appointments as well as rescheduled and canceled appointments. This regular meeting keeps both parties on the same page while continuing to build and maintain momentum in your specific MSAs.

Tools

Having the right tool at your disposal helps get a job done faster, and more importantly, it gets it done right. Unfortunately, sometimes we give our ISAs the wrong tool and it's like giving someone a spoon instead of a shovel to dig a hole. It just makes doing the job and getting the results you want that much harder to do.

The same philosophy applies to running your inside sales department. You want your ISA to be on the phone making calls and not spending time dealing with ineffective CRMs, dialers, phone systems, computers, and lead generation platforms. If any one of these tools is not ample enough for the job your ISA needs to do, they are putting you and your ISA at a disadvantage. That doesn't mean you have to have the absolute most expensive technology...it just means you need to have the best tool for the job.

Your Inside Sales Toolbox

There is no shortage of technology for you to choose from when arming your inside sales department with the tools it needs to succeed. Here's a brief overview of the tools you need to run your sales desk effectively, without emptying your wallet:

- **Dialer**: Your ISA's incidence of contact is directly related to how many people there are for him/her to call and how fast he/she can get to them. Having a good dialer allows for your ISA to get in touch with the largest number of people in the shortest period of time. Ideally, you'll want an extremely efficient dialer (one that runs quickly), as that will usually help you get the best results. A one-line dialer, while not optimal, is still more effective than hand dialing.

  If you have a dialer that automatically leaves messages while the next number is being dialed or provides a slydial feature (where the number is called and a message is left without ringing the prospect's phone) you'll be able to dial and contact a significant number of prospects each day and even get some inbound calls at the same time.

  Before you settle on a dialer, do your research to determine that it's the best for your specific needs. Having a dialer in place for your ISA to use just because you like it isn't the right reason to keep using it. Ask yourself this question whether you have a dialer in place or are ready to purchase one: "Is this dialer the absolute best for my specific situation and goals?" If you don't get a resounding "Yes," it's not the right dialer and you shouldn't use it.

- **Computer**: When choosing a computer for your business, the desktop that costs $275 in the Sunday sales circular is not your best choice. You need a desktop—an actual business computer— that will allow you to run your CRM, dialer, email, calendar, and a few other programs all at the same time...without dimming the lights. A good business computer requires a better-than-average processor and enough RAM to expand as necessary. Storage isn't a huge requirement and neither is an amped-up graphics display. You're looking for simplicity and speed in processing so your ISA can move between software programs with ease.

Please note: You could have the best computer on the face of the planet and it will be handicapped by poor Internet connection speed. Before you go out and drop some cash on computer equipment, test your connection speed at www.speedtest.net.

- **Phone System**: Your ISA's job is to work on the phone all day, so having a good quality phone system is a no-brainer. If you work out of the office of a major, regional, or local real estate brand, you'll want to make sure that the phone system can and will allow you to make calls through a dialer and have those calls recorded. These are a must in order for you to get solid results and to train your ISA on an ongoing basis. You'll also want to make sure there isn't an additional cost, per dial, to run your inside sales department using their system. If these things can't happen, you should look into your own phone server and phones.

- **CRM**: Your Customer Relationship Management (CRM) system is the foundation on which your business and inside sales department are run. It's where all the data and notes for every lead you have are stored. When it comes to your CRM, it needs to have enough bells and whistles to allow you to maintain excellent records and seamlessly communicate with each lead via phone, text, email, and direct mail.

The good news is that many lead generation platforms have robust enough back ends to suffice as the main CRM for your business. As an aside, your CRM must be fast enough to keep up with the demands of your ISA as he/she dials and dispositions hundreds of leads per day.

Your CRM should also have the capability of providing you with a variety of reports to help you track and monitor your results. The reporting function should be easy to use and you should be able to run a number of searches to see, in real time, the results of the various lead sources you're calling. You want the reports to tell you the stories that are going to help you make adjustments to fine tune all of your lead sources, processes, systems, training, and personnel to achieve optimal and consistent results day in and day out.

Data Warehouse: Your CRM is important to the daily management of your leads, but it's not the most important part of creating a predictable pipeline of listing business that you can scale as large as you want. In order to scale your business and build long-term predictability, you need to have a data warehouse of leads with detailed information about each lead.

According to Informatica, *"Data warehouses use a different design from standard operational databases. The latter are optimized to maintain strict accuracy of data in the moment by rapidly updating real-time data. Data warehouses, by contrast, are designed to give a long-range view of data over time. They trade off transaction volume and instead specialize in data aggregation."*

The ability to review the quality of data and the results that have been achieved through the data you have provides you with the foresight you need to plan and grow your business. A good data warehouse not only illustrates past trends in your business, it can help forecast future opportunities and/or pitfalls to help you with making decisions for the future.

Your data warehouse is the cornerstone of scaling your business as big as you want to grow it.

- **Lead Generation Platforms**: Your ISA needs a variety of lead sources in order to fill his/her pipeline with seller prospects (and listing appointments). They should be inclusive of, but not limited to: expireds, withdrawns, FSBOs, circle prospecting leads, and home evaluation leads.

Your goal when picking lead providers is to first ensure that the leads are good and have good data associated with them. Lead sources that provide you with bad names, phone numbers, emails, and addresses waste your money and your ISA's time. Be sure your lead providers offer the highest-quality leads so your ISA can have a high contact rate to set more and better appointments for you.

Second, make sure they provide a means for you to upload their leads to your CRM as flawlessly as possible. Your ISA needs to be able to access all the data easily and have all the phone numbers available for each lead to have the best chance of contacting that lead.

There may be other tools that you can add to your toolbox, but the ones listed above are mandatory if your ISA is going to hit home runs for you. As well, each of these tools is an investment and as such, can be measured for effectiveness in getting you the results that you want and need. It's important that you conduct regular reviews of your tools to ensure that you're getting the best return on your investment.

Lastly, as I mentioned earlier, you don't need to spend a ton of money on your tools, but you do need to spend enough to get tools that will support your ISA's efforts on a daily basis and put him/her in position to succeed.

One last thing regarding tools.

You can add efficiency, save money and increase your ISA's productivity by using tools that are integrated with each other. For instance, as I mentioned earlier, some lead generation platforms have a solid CRM on their back end that can be used as your main CRM. This combination of resources makes lead generation and uploading pretty seamless and shortens your and your ISA's learning curve when using the system.

As well, if you can find a lead generation platform with a dialer (or one that integrates all three tools in one), your inside sales department will spend less time learning and using multiple tools and more time making calls and setting appointments. The economies of scale that fully integrated tools gives you and your ISA are immeasurable. You can save money on tools, lead generation, and labor costs, it becomes easier for everyone in your organization to work with it and your ISA can set more appointments for you on a week-over-week basis...all of which lead to the creation of the predictable pipeline we've been discussing.

You can get a look at our tool audit checklists and metrics by going to www.insidesalespredictability.com/toolaudit

Systems

The last part of weaving the fabric of the inside sales platform together are your systems. According to Charles Gilkey from the visionary group, Productive Flourishing, there is a difference between systems and processes: "*A process is a conceptual sequence of events that enables people in a business to do what they do. Systems are what's used to execute the process.*"

When applying systems to your real estate organization, you need to remember that systems support processes that support people. In some cases the systems are actual hardware and technology and in other cases, they are means by which things are done within a process. For the purpose of our discussion, we're going to focus on the latter.

Now, there are a number of systems that you can employ within your inside sales department, but the three listed below are some of the most important in helping your ISA to hit it dead solid perfect each day:

1. **Feedback Loop**: In most cases, your ISAs are not going to have a lot of experience on listing appointments and your OSAs aren't

going to have a lot of experience working the phones for 500 dials a day. As a result of that, it's important for the ISAs and the OSAs to give and receive feedback to and from each other on a regular basis. Having this system in place helps your ISA improve his/her appointment-setting skills and it helps build your OSA's confidence in your ISA. Additionally, it helps the ISA put the OSA in position to have an amazing listing presentation with a high probability of securing the listing.

The End of Day report provided to you by your ISA can play a huge part in giving them and the OSA some great ground to cover within this feedback loop. The daily reporting of numbers by your ISA will show the OSA trends and details as it they pertain to the OSAs listing appointments and pipeline.

I spoke earlier about the ISA/OSA meeting to discuss the OSA's pipeline, but I chose to cover it again because I believe this part of the sales process is just that important.

2. **Progressive Profiling**: If you recall, I discussed the importance of having your ISA take notes in your CRM for the purposes of building strong relationships with prospects and clients as well as to help other team members stay up to date on what's happening with their pipeline. There is a specific system that is used to take and keep notes based on the successive conversations your ISA is having with a prospect, and it's called progressive profiling.

Through progressive profiling, your ISA gathers pertinent

information—information related to both the home sale as well as personal—from each contact with the prospect. Each time contact is made, more information is gathered and rapport is strengthened. The goal is for your ISA to gather enough information each time on the phone to be increasingly more effective in influencing the prospect to move forward with setting an appointment. The key is to take good enough notes with key data to be used on the next call(s) without 1) sounding like a broken record and saying the same thing on each call, and 2) writing a book every time you take notes from a call. The end result of this system is more qualified listing appointments with sellers who are very open to working with you because the relationship between your ISA and them has been built strongly by your ISA.

3. **Checks and Balances**: Once you have the process for dealing with the life cycle of a lead nailed down, you need a system to track the inflow of leads and what happens with each of them. The system must account for each lead source, the total number of leads from each source, the cost per lead from each source, how many contacts are made to each lead source, the total number of appointments from each lead source, and then the total number of leads from each lead source. In addition to that, your system also needs to adjust the reporting to give you seasonal results as well as results by ISA and OSA so you can see how seasonality and personnel affect the overall results.

Having this system in place helps you determine which lead source(s) to continue using, which one(s) to stop using and if your team members are converting at the level they should be. This will lead to huge savings in time and money and help you determine if you have a leads problem, training problem, and/or a people problem...and put you in a position to solve the problem.

CHAPTER 5 - PROSPECTS, NURTURES, AND LEADS

"Prospects equal options. Master prospecting and you will be the master of your sales destiny."
— Tibor Shanto,
CEO Renbor Sales Solutions

Not all prospects are created equally. Not all sales calls are good sales calls. Not all lead sources are good lead sources. When it comes to providing your ISA with solid leads to turn into prospects, nurtures, and appointments, you have to be strategic with where you invest your time, energy, and money in order to get the best results. What is the outcome? Where do you want listings? In what price range do you want to have a presence? Where are the proverbial "fish biting" so you can get consistent sales coming into your business? What's the best way to convert different lead sources when they come through the door?

Having a solid sales funnel in place will help you answer many of these questions on your way to achieving great results.

Internet marketing website, Convert With Content, defines a sales funnel as:

> "[A] marketing system. It's the 'ideal' process you intend your customers to experience as they go from Prospect to Lead to Customer to Repeat Buyer. Sales funnels have been around much longer than web marketing, but the online world is the best thing to ever happen to sales funnels because websites and email marketing make sales funnels easier to build.
>
> The purpose of a funnel is to make things easier and cleaner. When you put fresh, new oil in your car for example, you don't want oil leaking all over your engine. So what do you do? You use a funnel to increase the likelihood that all (or most) of the oil will go straight to its destination. Sales funnels work the same way—they help you avoid "leaking" (or losing) potential customers.
>
> The important thing is to think strategically about the results you want before you plunk down a bunch of cash. It will save you a lot of time, money, and headaches, and more importantly, it will help you establish a solid lead generation strategy and a predictable pipeline for your business."

Stages of Leads

Before I dig into leads more deeply, let's talk a bit about the stages in which a lead can fall and what that stage means to your ISA as he/she makes calls each day. The stages are as follows:

Suspects: A suspect is really just another name for a lead. Your ISA only knows that this person likely has a home and may be open to selling at some point in the future. No warranties or guarantees... just a name, number, address (and maybe an email). Targeted lead generation will help make your suspects more likely to fall into the next stage.

Prospects: A suspect becomes a prospect only after your ISA makes contact. Once contact is made, the quality of the prospect is now known and it's up to your ISA to determine whether or not the lead should remain a prospect or be marked as lost. If the lead is marked lost, it doesn't mean it's lost for good. Your ISA, based on details from the sales call, can choose to make a call in the future to check in and confirm his/her instincts as to whether or not the opportunity is legit.

The minimum standard for a prospect is for him/her to be ready, willing, and able to sell, and if you remember, he/she should be wanting to sell within the next 90 days. To make sure the prospect is even more qualified, he/she should be selling in a target neighborhood/subdivision with good turnover, desired price range (no less than a certain amount of money) and not be listed with or committed to another agent. The reason for doing this is two-fold. First, probability plays a role in growing your business exponentially. You want your ISA calling leads where the prospects are more likely or probable to sell. You only have so much time, energy, and money, so it makes sense to use it where you're likely to get the greatest return on your investment.

Second, although It may seem like you are excluding a number of listing opportunities by being so targeted, doing so helps foster predictability. If you start with a standard set of outcomes that you can track on a consistent basis, you can review reports regularly to determine if you're reaching them. Certainly, there's no rule saying the outcomes can't change from time to time. It's just that you want and need them to be uniform so you can use your systems and processes in the same manner to hit them consistently. Once you do this, the numbers will help you see what needs to happen to get the same results on a day-over-day basis.

Follow-up: At this level, your ISA doesn't feel that the timing and motivation are where they're supposed to be to set the lead as a nurture or an appointment. He/she does, however, feel that there is a potential opportunity for the prospect to become one in the future. The follow-up can happen later that day or it can be a year or more later. Ideally, you want to confine follow-ups to prospects who you feel are moderately serious about making a move.

Nurture: Once your ISA has vetted the the prospect properly and determined that it meets the criteria I detailed earlier, he/she will mark it as a nurture in the CRM. A nurture can be selling in one day or one year, and your ISA will need to identify the lead as a nurture only when he/she can't get an appointment with the him/her. When that happens, your ISA needs to schedule a next-action date for a follow-up call that should occur a little less than half the time prior to when the nurture is ready to sell.

Additionally, your ISA will also set a nurture date in your CRM for the date he/she understands when the seller would be willing to sell. Setting these two dates allows your ISA to stay on top of next-action dates for follow-up calls and nurture dates for when the seller is going to sell. This strategy also allows you to do some forecasting of opportunities for the future not only to see how many potential listing opportunities you have each month based on actual nurture dates, but also to build the foundation of your predictability pipeline.

Nurtures are the key to a predictable, repeatable business model. By creating and building relationships with nurtures, your ISA is setting the stage for consistent, daily listing appointments for your business. And by adding regular follow-up strategies like handwritten notes, monthly market updates, emails, texts, and other forms of contact, you are virtually guaranteeing a steady pipeline of loyal, ready-to-sell sellers.

Lastly, there are two types of nurtures: Hard and Soft.

Hard nurtures meet the criteria that we've discussed here in this section and in other parts of this book. They are not only motivated, and willing to work with you, but also they want to sell in the next year. Their timing and motivation is clear and easy to get your head around.

Soft nurtures are sellers that have mentioned they are wanting to sell, but they don't meet the criteria for a nurture motivated to sell in the next year. It could be two or more years away. Soft nurtures will get your market trends report and then a small number of well-placed calls over the next couple of years until their timing and motivation are determined to be more specific and closer to the next year or less.

Appointment: I covered this in detail earlier. Just remember that a proper appointment has a date, a time, a completed SCI and it has been put into the OSA's calendar and the OSA confirms that he/she can go. Also, be sure to have the ISA call to confirm the appointment prior to sending the OSA out for the meeting. Unconfirmed appointments often lead to nobody being home when the agent shows up. If the time set aside to meet the seller doesn't meet all those criteria, it's not an appointment.

Go to www.insidesalespredictability.com/leadstages to get a more detailed explanation and description of the various lead stages.

Leads

When you survey the landscape of lead providers in the real estate universe, you'll see that there are multiple providers of seller and buyer leads. Many of these companies offer similar products with various bells and whistles and at first glance, they can all look the same. Oftentimes, these companies confuse form with function in an effort to sell you their product and they do this by focusing on all the ancillary benefits to using their product instead of on the most important part of what they offer—the lead.

Dialers, lead delivery methods, texting ability, slydial, auto-generated emails, etc., are all great and helpful in converting leads. Unfortunately, it's the leads that matter and if they're not good, no number of added features will make them any better. Your concern should be with the lead augmentation and what the company does to provide you with good, clean, detailed data.

Lead augmentation is nothing more than list cleansing that provides you with clean, detailed data about a specific lead. By augmenting their leads, good data providers get rid of inaccurate data to help your ISA be more efficient and effective in working the list of leads you get from them. Remember, the lower the quality of leads you get, the more work your ISA has to put in to get in contact with them. The outcome of this strategy is not favorable: You spend more money on labor and leads, but get fewer appointments and sales; not what I would necessarily call the formula for success.

You must take the time to vet your lead sources and make sure that what they provide is in line with what you're looking to accomplish and more importantly, that they can get you the results you want with the quality of leads they provide.

Again, not any lead generation platform or lead will do.

What Makes a Good Lead?

Now that we're clear on the importance of having good leads, what is it, exactly, that makes them good? Fortunately, the answer is pretty simple. Good leads have the following qualities:

- **Detailed Contact Information**: The basics—name, phone number, address, email—are all very important. Good lead providers will augment their lead lists to get you multiple phone numbers, additional potential addresses, spouse names, and any other de-tails that will make it easy for your ISA to either get in contact with the right person or find a way to get in contact with him/her.

127

- **Accurate information**: Details are great, but they need to be the right details. Lead augmentation is key here. The better the leads, the better job the lead provider has done with aggregating and scrubbing the data. That's not to say every lead is going to be perfect, but you want the best contact information you can get in order for the rest of the process to work.

- **Quantity Matters**: Your ISA is going to need a decent daily allocation of phone numbers to call so you can create your predictable pipeline of sales. On average, we give our ISAs about 400 individual records per day with each record having about two to three numbers (800 to 1200 numbers total). The daily target for our ISAs is 500 dials. Five hundred dials per day puts them in position to make enough contacts for them to meet (and sometimes exceed) their daily nurture and appointment goal. If your lead generation platform(s) can't get you access to that many contacts on a regular basis, you'll want to reconsider using them.

One point of note: It's obvious that you won't get 400 expireds, withdrawns, FSBOs, and market evaluation leads the first day you get rolling. You're going to have to build up those data sources over time. And while you can and should get access to past expireds that go back at least five years, you're going to need to build up the lead data for the other sources you're going to be calling. Having a good data provider for circle prospecting will help with rapidly achieving the large quantity of leads you'll need.

One of the things I've observed by mentoring so many real estate agents over the last 15 years is that many of them (and I was like this at one point myself) hold onto lead sources that they either aren't working or aren't getting good leads from way longer than they should. I can't explain the phenomenon, but I believe that we do that because we don't want to admit we made a mistake. I also know we have the belief that one lead converted to a sale could lead to a huge payday and justify all the lost expenses we incur on these types of lead sources.

The reality of the matter is this: Those lead sources rarely, if ever, come through either over time or in a pinch with a huge sale. And, long as you've worked the leads diligently, you can and should get rid of any lead generation platform that isn't providing you the kind of leads I've discussed in this chapter.

When it comes to lead generation, categorizing and then following up with the leads, it's vital to measure twice—and maybe even three times—before you cut. In other words, perform your due diligence prior to buying. Make sure that you see how the platform works and how detailed the leads are. In addition to that, get the names of at least three other people who have used the data source and can show you in black and white that they've converted the leads into actual sales. Unless you have a huge pile of expendable cash, it's not ideal for you to be the alpha or beta tester of a new lead generation platform.

You want to use proven and tested lead sources.

Once you've targeted the areas and price range you want to work and you're sure you have the best lead sources, you must monitor the quality and quantity of leads that come from each source. From there, you absolutely must track and review your results.

You'll want to measure the quantity of good numbers vs. bad numbers, the number of people who are contacted that are actually the homeowner vs. those who are not, the number of nurtures that are created and even the number of appointments that are set. Knowing all of these details are key in getting the best lead source for your business.

If you're not willing to do that, there's really no need to even buy the leads or set up an inside sales department. You'd be better off taking that money and going to Vegas to hit the craps table. Predictability only comes as a result of this level of diligence with the life cycle of your leads.

CHAPTER 6 - MANAGING YOUR ISAs

"There are only three measurements that tell you nearly everything you need to know about your organization's overall performance: employee engagement, customer satisfaction, and cash flow. It goes without saying that no company, small or large, can win over the long run without energized employees who believe in the mission and understand how to achieve it."

– Jack Welch,
former CEO of GE

If you've ever seen a late-night infomercial, you've likely seen Ron Popeil promoting his world-famous *Showtime Rotisserie Oven* on television. In the presentation, Popeil puts roasts, chickens, and just about every other meat on the planet in the oven to show how "hands-off" the oven is in cooking meat to the perfect temperature. Once the meat is in the machine, he shuts the door, turns the timer, looks at the crowd and shouts "Set it!" At that point, the crowd shouts "And forget it!" and they erupt in thunderous applause.

It's kind of an obscure analogy for a book about inside sales, but it makes my point. "Set it and forget it" is not only the tagline for Popeil's rotisserie oven, it's also the management style of many real estate agents with ISAs.

Historically, many real estate agents who have been successful in selling homes often seek to build a team as a means of gaining leverage to expand their business. Unfortunately, the skills that make us amazing sales people don't necessarily translate well into become excellent managers.

In fact, because the skill sets of, and core requirements to be, a rockstar salesperson are so different than those possessed by great managers, rockstar salespeople often hire an ISA (sometimes anyone) to fill the spot...and then do little, if anything to guide their ISA or give him/her a track on which to run.

The results of this approach are often disastrous: The salesperson, usually unintentionally, does little if anything to help the ISA succeed and as a result, the ISA feels lost and frustrated, doesn't see the vision of what you're looking to accomplish and decides to leave not long after being hired.

When this happens, you don't go back to square one, you go back to the square that's before square one. I say this because you have to take time away from dollar-productive activities to assume the duties your now-ex-employee was going to handle for you. As well, you have to take even more time out of your schedule to find another person to fill the position.

Worst of all is that if you don't change the way you're addressing the situation, you're doomed to experience the exact same thing with your next ISA and create a vicious cycle of failure for yourself.

The good news in all of this is that when you do hire, onboard, and train an ISA properly, you can actually give him/her a decent amount of autonomy in doing his/her job, which will free you up to list homes with white hot abandon. This doesn't mean you can abandon your ISA and see them only on birthdays and holidays, you still have to track their progress, give them feedback and manage their activities. You just don't have to spend every waking moment doing it.

To get some great strategies on managing your business and your ISAs, check out the weekly Face-to-Face podcasts with my partner Jay Kinder and I. You can get access to them at www.facetofacepodcast.com

Let's take a look at some of the key management strategies you need to employ to get your ISA up to speed, producing consistently, and in hopefully rare cases, out the door when he/she doesn't get the job done.

Getting Your ISA on Pace

Pace is defined as the speed or rate at which something happens, changes, or develops. When it comes to your ISA, the pace we're talking about is the consistent number of dials, contacts, nurtures, and appointments he/she produces on a daily basis. There's a required target for each of these and your ISA is on pace when he/she hits that target with regularity.

In Chapter 1, I talked about how the ISA's income would likely be salary only for the first 120 days since it takes time to build a pipeline and get some sales to come out of the other end. The first half of this span is called the ISA's ramp period and during this time, your ISA is going through the 84-day onboarding plan and learning and mastering your processes, systems, scripts, and dialogues. The goal is to get your ISA on pace—hitting the targets you've set for them—by the end of the ramp. As long as you've made a great hire, followed the onboarding strategy and put the ISA in position to succeed, he/she should be on point and getting the results you want and need from within about 60 days.

At the beginning of the ramp (which also coincides with the 84-day onboarding plan), you will set the daily, weekly, and monthly targets for your ISA and gain his/her agreement on hitting them. You will also review with him/her your expectations for time on the phone, breaks, as well as following the processes and systems you've created.

Your initial set of instructions and expected outcomes need to be crystal clear from your ISA's first day to ensure that there is no confusion as to what you want your ISA to do. This is important for two reasons: 1) You have invested a lot of time and money into getting your ISA to this point and you want him/her to succeed wildly, and 2) at the end of that 84-day onboarding period, it should be apparent as to whether or not your ISA is going to make it or not and you don't want there to be any doubt about keeping this person or letting him/her go. The best-case scenario, however, is that your ISA is crushing at that point (and again, he/she should be if you've done what you're supposed to do up front).

The First 30 Days

Our targets for our ISAs during the first 30 days are to make 500 outbound dials, capture 2.5 to 3 nurtures per day and get roughly .5 appointments per day. With an average of 22 workdays per month, your ISA should snag about 55 nurtures and 10 to 11 appointments the first 30 days on the job. If it's more, awesome. If it's less, it's not necessarily time to panic. It may just mean you need to make some adjustments, which will likely come in the form of improving the skill and effort from your ISA.

Now, it should be your goal to get your ISA on the phone as soon as possible during the first 30 days. Yes, onboarding and training are super important, but nothing will help him/her craft the battle-tested, bulletproof demeanor he/she needs to perform like a grizzled veteran than being on live sales calls. By employing the "I do it, we do it, you do it" training strategy, you should be able to get your ISA on the phone and swimming in the deep end of the pool very quickly.

One last thing about the first 30 days of the ramp: You're going to get some bad appointments in the beginning. Your ISA is going to be excited to get you in the front door of a few houses and in his/her naivete, will likely misunderstand something a seller says or miss a step in the process. This is going to lead to meeting with sellers for a couple of appointments that will have you shaking your head when you're done. Please know that this is a good thing. It's all part of the process and these weaker appointments will give you opportunities to provide your ISA with solid feedback and learning opportunities to improve his/her game dramatically over a short period of time. Create feedback loops to provide your ISA with the information he/she needs to become better on the phone, faster. These feedback loops will also give your ISA an opportunity to share any sticking points he/she if facing that you can resolve for him/her.

When this does happen—and it will happen—remember to be hard on the problem and not on the person. Your ISA is new and knows only a fraction of what you know. He/she will need your kind but firm guidance and support until things are up and running at full speed.

The Next 30 Days

Once the first half of the ramp period is over, you should have a very good idea of your ISA's strengths and the areas where he/she needs improvement. In extreme cases, you may have to let your ISA go because your gut (and the results) tell you that this person just isn't going to make it. It's unlikely that letting the ISA go will need to happen, you just need to be prepared mentally and emotionally that it is a possibility. It's also possible to know that you've got a blue chipper at this stage of the game, too.

Most likely, however, your ISA will be on point and ready to get to the next phase of the process. From tracking and monitoring your ISA's progress during the first 30 days, you will be able to give him/her the necessary feedback to be in position to fully ramped by the end of the 84-day onboarding period.

For this second half of the ramp, some of your ISA's targets will go up. Dials stay at 500, but the nurture requirement increases to 3.5 per day and appointments go to one per day. Using the same 22-day month as your basis, the monthly nurture goal is 75 to 80 and appointments increase to 20 to 25. Nurtures should take a huge upswing at this point in your ISA's growth process.

These numbers are realistic and very achievable as long as you follow what I've laid out for you in this book. However, to ensure that you help keep your ISA on pace on a month-over-month basis, there are some things you're going to need do from a managerial standpoint on a consistent basis. Your consistent support and tracking will be key in establishing the predictability you are seeking for your business.

Keeping Your ISA on Pace

Keeping in mind that you can't foster ongoing success within your inside sales department with a set-it-and-forget-it mentality, you need to check in regularly with your ISA. By doing this, you provide him/her with the accountability and direction they desperately want and need to succeed in their job. And while we're not advocating micromanagement in any way, shape, or form, we are saying that there are a standard set of meetings and activities in which you should engage to keep your ISA on pace.

Dale Carnegie is famous for saying: "*You have to inspect what you expect, because people respect what you inspect.*" Here's a quick peek at what we recommend you do regularly to stay on top of what your

ISA is doing as well as to keep both of you engaged in the entire inside sales process:

- **Daily Huddle**: Business optimization expert, Verne Harnish, loves the daily huddle or daily adrenaline meeting, as he calls it. According to Harnish, the daily huddle is the "one [thing] that is non-negotiable" in your business. A daily huddle is comprised of three things: what's up/good news, daily numbers, and where are you stuck. For the huddle, all team members stand in a circle and share good news first. The next time around, numbers are reviewed and discussed and the last time around, any choke points and challenges are addressed.

  The are many benefits to the daily huddle:
  1. It's a great way to strengthen team unity and get the day started off on a positive note.
  2. It's a passive accountability strategy because the numbers that the ISAs generate the day before are covered out loud, in front of the group.
  3. It stokes the competitive fires for the ISAs and OSAs on your team because everyone sees the daily results.
  4. It gives you, the leader, a platform to keep your finger on the pulse of what's happening in your organization.

  Your huddle should last about 15 minutes, 20 minutes tops, be organized, and most importantly, it should be done every day—Monday through Friday—without fail. Even if you can't be there, make sure the huddle occurs. Predictability is a direct result of consistency and it starts with your daily huddle.

- **One-on-one Meetings**: You and your ISA need to sit down, once per week, for a 20- to 30-minute one-on-one meeting. This meeting is your opportunity to give your ISA formal feedback on the job he/she is doing. When you meet, you need to review his/her performance from the prior week, whether or not he/she is on pace and what changes need to be made, if any, to help him/her stay on pace. It's also an opportunity for you to connect with your ISA and build continued rapport, which helps your ISA come to you with feedback you need to help him/her while making your ISA more receptive to your feedback and guidance.

Once per quarter, you'll do a quarterly review with your ISA to illustrate how his/her month-over-month and quarter-over-quarter are stacking up. As long as you're having weekly one-on-one meetings, there really shouldn't be any surprises during the quarterly review. The review should be used as means of giving your ISA perspective on his/her growth and accomplishments. As well, you should use the review to continue coaching and training your ISA and to help him/her set and reach goals as part of your strategy to help them grow personally and professionally. Your investment of time in both the one-on-one meetings and reviews will pay great dividends in the form of great results from a loyal, hard-working ISA.

- **Call Review Sessions**: Since scripts and dialogues, tone of voice, and syntax are so important to influencing prospects over the phone, they need to be reviewed regularly by you and your ISA in the form of recorded call sessions. Next to making live calls, listening to what you're saying, how you're saying it, and when you're saying it are extremely effective in shortening the learning curve for you and your ISA. Many people don't like to listen to the sound of their own voice, but all ISAs need to if they are to become experts at selling and relationship building over the phone.

You are the best salesperson on your team; you know better than anyone else how a good sales call is supposed to go. When you listen to a recording of your ISA's sales calls, you can give him/her immediate feedback as you pick up on mistakes that are made during the sales process. Your ISA, in doing this with you, will not only use that feedback to make real-time adjustments in his/her skill set and effort when making calls, he/she will also be able to start picking up on mistakes when they listen to the calls with you (and even by themselves) in the future. Call review sessions are a key element of grooming your ISA for excellence.

- **Reviewing Notes in CRM**: Letting your ISA do things the wrong way without making consistent adjustments along the way provides a pathway for bad habits to be formed—bad habits that could hamper his/her ability to do the best possible job for you. One area where bad habits can form quickly and easily is in his/her note-taking skills and efforts. I spoke earlier about progressive profiling and the importance of having good notes in building relationships over the phone. There's really no substitute for good notes for that part of the appointment- setting process. And by reviewing your ISA's notes—at least weekly—you can give the proper guidance to ensure that the notes are clean and easy to understand and read. It's especially important because at some point, the lead will be turned into an appointment and you'll need to use those notes to properly prepare for your presentation.

- **Review Completion of Daily Tasks**: A good CRM will provide everyone who uses it reminders when tasks that they set are due to be completed. Our CRM is no different. The ISAs at our office get reminders of tasks due that day in their portal in the CRM. Virtually all of the tasks are next-action dates for follow-up calls to either set an appointment or move a seller along in the sales process. Since these tasks represent calls that are more likely to turn into appointments, it's crucial that each of them is attended to on the day for which they are scheduled for completion. In the world of inside sales, being even a minute late can mean the difference between getting an appointment and not getting one.

  I'll say it again for emphasis: These task reminders are usually for calls with prospects that your ISA has been building a relationship with for any period over the last year. These tasks represent a better quality opportunity than virtually any new lead you give to your ISA to call. You and your ISA cannot let these tasks go unattended to, as it is literally like throwing money away.

- **Autopsies**: My business partner, Jay Kinder, loves talking about lessons learned. He really believes that you grow the most when you look back at decisions you made, and actions you took, to find the hidden lessons that are there to learn. I agree with this philosophy and have applied it to the listing process at our company.

Each time an OSA goes out on a listing appointment and doesn't get the listing, he/she is required to complete a listing autopsy that asks 21 questions about the listing process and how he/she feels the listing presentation went. It's super helpful and it lets us know where the disconnects are in our systems and processes as well as where the holes are in the OSA's and ISA's skill sets. The feedback is absolutely invaluable.

Here are some of the questions from the listing autopsy:
- Did I follow the sales cycle and process?
- Did I relate my products or service benefits to the needs and wants of the prospect?
- Did I control the interview and presentation?
- Did I handle all objections?
- Did I close at least five times before letting the prospect go?

In order to get consistent results, it's super important to schedule all of these events and activities with regular times and dates. When you and your ISA both know that these meetings are coming, there's less of a chance for poor performance to take root.

Grab a copy of our listing appointment autopsy here - www.insidesalespredictability.com/autopsy

Tony Robbins says that true transformation only exists on the other side of complete and total honesty. Our autopsies provide our sales organization with an honest assessment of the larger piece of our

144

appointment-setting and listing process. The benefit of being open to this feedback allows us improve faster and better in our quest create an even more predictable pipeline of listing appointments and sales.

Fish or Cut Bait

Your goal when you hire what you to believe to be a legit ISA is not to fire that him/her; that is unless you are Ebenezer Scrooge, of course. Unfortunately, no matter how closely you follow the process, one or two of your ISA hires over time just aren't going to work out. The question I usually get when agents are at the crossroads of fish or cut bait is: "How do you decide if the ISA should stay or go?"

The decision is never an easy one to make, but it can be simple to determine if it's the right call. It's not easy because letting someone go from your business affects his/her life and the lives of his/her loved ones. Conversely, it's simple because it should be clear between 30 and 60 days—because of the metrics and activities you've been tracking—as to whether or not your ISA is going to make it. Essentially, your gut will tell you and the results will speak for themselves.

That said, here are three things—in addition to the fact that the ISA isn't a core value fit or doesn't show up regularly—you can look for if you're faced with the tough decision of letting someone go:

1. **Numbers are Lagging**: You've set daily, weekly, and monthly targets for your ISAs and you've reviewed his/her results regularly in daily huddles, one-on-one meetings and quarterly reviews. Also, you've

given him/her a tremendous amount of feedback along the way, so your ISA should have had multiple opportunities get and stay on pace. That said, if your ISA is consistently at less than 80 percent of pace after 60 days, it's time to let him/her go. The only caveat here is that there have been some extenuating circumstances that have kept your ISA from being on pace, you would reconsider. Some of those circumstances would be: 1) an unexpected death in the family, 2) a health issue that kept your ISA out for a couple of weeks, or 3) if your leads, processes, systems, or technology prevented your ISA from doing the job you hired him/her to do. Absent a circumstance like this popping up, you would be best served to let your ISA go.

2. **Effort is Lagging**: Being a full-time ISA can be challenging at times, there's no question about that. If your ISA needs breaks between call sessions during the day, by all means let him/her charge his/her batteries. There is, however, a difference between being tired and needing a break and simply not putting forth the best effort. You see, your ISA's growth in the inside sales department is the compound effect of taking the feedback you give to him/her—and using that feedback to work hard at becoming a little bit better each day. If there is a point at which you're giving your ISA feedback to resolve his/her issues on the phone and he/she stops putting forth the effort to make improvements, it's time to let your ISA go. You can teach your ISA just about anything he/she would want to know to be successful, but you can't make him/her want to put forth the effort to improve daily. That's something that comes from the inside. Once your ISA seems to have given up...it's time for you to give up on your ISA.

3. **Skills and Attitude Are Poor**: This issue really stems from lack of effort. You laid out the expectations for your ISA the first day that he/she started working for you. Skills mastery, strong effort, note taking, and following processes and systems were all minimum requirements for success. If you see your ISA not working to improve his/her skills, displaying a poor attitude, not taking your feedback to heart, keeping insufficient notes in the CRM, and simply not doing what you ask him/her to do, it's definitely time for him/her to go. I've always lived by the philosophy that you give people every chance you can to succeed. If they don't use the opportunities I give them, then I subscribe to an entirely different philosophy: "If you can't change people, then you have to change people."

Time to Step Up

Managing your ISA is something that you should look at with anticipation and excitement. Not only do you have the opportunity to create a tremendous amount of leverage in your business, you also have the chance to impact another person's life and help make their dreams come true. The important thing to remember when bringing on an ISA is that you must make the commitment to putting him/her in position to succeed. That means you have a track on which he/she can run from the day you bring him/her on board for the rest of his/her time with you.

Also, systems and processes for feedback and accountability are absolute musts if you are ever going to help your ISA become independent and free yourself from the job of prospecting. In managing your ISAs in this fashion, you put yourself in position to either grow them into full-fledged phone salespeople with master-level savvy or thank them for their service and send them on their way in good conscience when they don't pan out.

CHAPTER 7 - REPORTING

"Without data, you're just another person with an opinion."
- W. Edwards Deming
Management consultant, Engineer, Consultant.

To implement a solid inside sales department, you must have an effective reporting, analytics, and data delivery system. Having one in place provides you with a means to easily consume vital metrics and data, which will in turn provide for some forward-thinking decision-making and help you build a predictable pipeline that will serve your business for years to come.

Distilling data and the having the proper reporting and analytic strategy boosts your ability to make more informed, real-time, numbers-based decisions.

With the right reporting, analytics and information in your hands, you can ensure the decisions you make will have a profound effect on your lead generation and conversion and ultimately, sales.

The merits of a strong reporting strategy include:

- Better, more targeted data
- Dramatically improved productivity
- Improved labor efficiency
- Improved analysis and decision-making
- Better communication between departments
- Significant cost savings over time on lead generation, labor, and technology

Proper reporting and the delivery of data can transform your company and explode the results you get in way less time than you would think. A number of data options are available, and by reviewing them and how they can align your overall real estate organization, you can assure success within your inside sales department (or any department for that matter). Here are some of the key reports and reporting mechanisms we use on a regular basis to make strategic decisions at our office.

You can get a look at some of the reports we generate by going to www.insidesalespredictability.com/dashboard.

Reports

- **ISA Targets**: Each day, we look at the individual and cumulative results of our ISA's required targets: dials, contacts, nurtures, and appointments. By reviewing this, we can literally work on the fly to correct any problems with lead flow, the tools, or our ISA's skills and efforts. The numbers always tell us a story and give us clues on what needs to be fixed or improved.

- **On-pace**: The main goal for the ISAs is to get on pace and then stay there. By producing an on-pace report, we can help them achieve those goals. The pace report can be run for our whole group of ISAs or segmented by ISA, OSA, or market service area in order for us to confirm the company, and our salespeople, are on pace. It also lets us know who is not on pace so we can do some targeted marketing and prospecting to get back on pace. This is a key distinction for this type of reporting. Rather than fumbling around and making wholesale changes to fix the problem, we use reporting to take a very targeted approach to fixing the problem area. It's a huge time and money saver for us.

- **Life Cycle of a Lead**: As I discussed earlier, it's important to track what happens to a lead from the time it hits your database to the time it turns into a closed sale. We run reports on lead sources to determine lead generation platform viability. We also run reports on lead conversion from contact to appointment, appointment kept and appointment not met, appointment to listing taken, and listing taken to homes sold. By looking at the full life cycle of a lead, we can make sure we are spending our time, energy, and money on the right lead sources on a day-over-day basis.

- **Average Cost Per Lead**: There are reasonable costs for different types of leads, and then there are unreasonable costs. A lead for circle prospecting should cost less than an expired and FSBO lead, somewhere around $.10 to $.15 per lead for a great lead source. Expired, withdrawn, and FSBO leads—including the platform— should cost a couple of hundred bucks per month. A home evaluation lead should cost more than all those lead sources, but really shouldn't cost more than $10 to $15 on average. The challenge for real estate business owners is that despite there being expected costs for certain lead types—even with seasonality figured in—costs per lead can get out of hand if they're not monitored. Running a regular report with the average costs per lead, by source and even by service area, can save you a tremendous amount of time and money.

- **Average Cost Per Nurture**: With nurtures being such a key factor in generating more listing appointments and sales, it's crucial to track the average cost on at least a monthly basis. Knowing your cost per nurture can help you determine both if your lead sources are on point and if your ISA is trained to identify and cultivate nurtures properly.

Reporting Mechanisms

- **Dashboard**: We have a dashboard where all of the dimensions and metrics we want to track and report on are stored. Dimensions are the categories that we're looking to track, i.e., leads source, dials, contacts, nurtures, appointments, etc., and metrics are the numbers that populate the row(s) of each dimension.

  The dashboard provides for an at-a-glance look at the dimensions and the associated core numbers we need to monitor and review on a daily basis for the purposes of decision making. The dashboard can be customized for different departments so that each department can have the dimensions and metrics that matter to it at the ready when needed.

Additionally, the dashboard gives us the ability to segment data a number of ways so that we can get a 360-degree look at the results we're getting to ensure that we're always focusing on the right things and giving priority to the issues that need the most attention.

- **Dialer Dashboard**: We also utilize a dialer dashboard that gives us access to the current and cumulative dial and contact information from our ISAs as well as the number of minutes they're spending on active calling. This updates in real time and gives us the information to see: 1) if the leads that the ISAs are calling are providing enough contacts for them to reach their daily targets, and 2) to see if the ISAs are putting in the requisite effort to reach their targets each day. Having access to this dashboard lets us respond immediately if we see something that's not right and step in to make adjustments as necessary.

- **Scoreboard**: Hanging smack-dab in the middle of the main wall in our call center is a large, flat-screen TV that updates the four target metrics we track for our ISAs. Each ISA's results flash and update every five seconds or so, with the results showing in descending order with the top performer in the first spot. It's a great tool to help keep the ISAs focused on their daily targets and it gives our team leaders the information they need to give pats on the back for great performances and feedback and guidance on improvements when numbers are lagging.

Running your business—and your sales desk—without tracking and reporting on the dimensions and metrics that are key to your success is like skiing down a black diamond run with a blindfold on: You might get moving forward at a pretty good clip, but you're gonna get hurt if you can't see where to make adjustments where the danger lurks. The smart thing to do is to put technology and systems in place that provide you with easy and detailed access to the data and analytics that you need to monitor on an ongoing basis. As well, you need to take the initiative to review your numbers, even daily in many cases, to prevent expenses from getting out of hand and keep your ISAs and OSAs on track to getting consistent and predictable results. You will likely experience a headache or two getting your reporting set up and working properly, but the pain you experience there will pale in comparison to the agony and torture you'll experience from a poorly run business that is losing money.

CONCLUSION

Setting up an inside sales department can seem like a daunting task, but it's not as overwhelming as you might think it would be when you have the right strategy for implementation in place. Plus, when you add the fact that listing sales generated by an ISA are usually less expensive than any direct mail marketing campaign you run, it's worth any challenges you might face to make it happen. And, once you get it up and running properly, an inside sales department is really the only mechanism you can use in your business to create long-term predictability.

Starting with the end in mind is always the key component to achieving your goals and this holds especially true with establishing inside sales within your business, but it's the hard work and good decisions you make at the beginning of your journey that will seal the deal for success. I know this because we've poured our hearts into every decision and action we've taken to set up the inside sales machine we have at our office.

In the beginning, hiring a solid ISA is going to get you great traction in moving the ball down the field to set yourself up to score. The person you choose to be your ISA is the single biggest decision you will make in creating a predictable pipeline of listing business. If the person you hire can't build relationships and influence prospects over the phone with consistency, no amount of leads, technology, training, or effort will be enough to get you into the end zone. You need someone who knows what they're doing on the phone and who you can groom into a hired gun in the real estate industry.

Getting your ISA up and running quickly will serve you well. The better job you do in following the 84-day onboarding plan and training your ISA on systems and skills, the faster you'll start getting results from that position on your team. More importantly, you'll have an individual on your team who will likely have some staying power to help knock the cover off the ball as you begin to grow your business exponentially. One of the key elements to making sure that you keep an ISA long term is having great structure in your business.

In our business, structure comes from having processes, systems, and technology that allow our ISAs to do their job well. These three instruments are the backbone of our inside sales business and we would certainly fail without having them solidly in place. By having them tight and easy to follow and work with, we are able to give our ISAs a significant amount of autonomy in doing their job. This frees our agents up to list more homes and it gives us the time we need to "steer the ship" and make adjustments, as necessary, to reach our goal faster and with more profitability.

By following the systems and processes we've created and by using the technology we make available for them, our ISAs are able to get solid and consistent results for our business. To ensure that they stay on track, we monitor a variety of dimensions and metrics on a daily, weekly, quarterly, and annual basis. The reporting we've set up is automated, clean, and easy to assimilate. Having access to the data our reporting provides us has saved us tens of thousands of dollars in expenses across our business model. More importantly, it is helping us position ourselves more and more strategically each day to create tremendous predictability in our business model.

As with all sales jobs, you need a reliable source of leads to contact in order to generate income for your business. It's important that you don't pick any old lead source to feed your inside sales machine. The leads and data sources you use will have a direct impact on how much money you make. Bad leads will not only cost you more money because you'll have to buy more of them, but they will also require more effort by your ISAs, increasing your labor costs, too. What's not mentioned anywhere in this book, but needs to be, is the huge opportunity cost that comes from using and sticking with inferior lead sources. Every call you make to weak leads and poor circle prospecting data is a call you won't be able to make to a blue chip opportunity. The compound effect of using and holding onto lead generation platforms that just don't get it done can be astronomically harmful over time.

Lastly, if you've not created a solid nurture strategy for your business, you are missing out on the next biggest factor in establishing a predictable pipeline of listings for yourself. Nurtures are the next best things to referral business and they can be almost as cost effective. The best part about nurtures is that you can put your finger on the pulse of sellers in your marketplace and know with a high degree of certainty when they are ready to make a move. And, because you are filling your pipeline continually with nurtures whom you are regularly building and strengthening relationships, you'll be able to set better listing appointments that have a much higher probability of turning into a listing and then a sale.

Elon Musk once said, *"If something's important enough, you should try. Even if the probable outcome is failure."*

Hiring an ISA is an important piece of the puzzle in making you the true CEO of your organization. For most agents, that's why they became real estate agents: to be their own boss and create an enterprise that would allow them to come and go as they please and take care of their family for generations to come. Knowing this to be true, I don't think hiring an ISA is something you should try to do, though. I think it's something you should do, period. I can assure you that when you do... the probable outcome will be success.

- - - - -